The Creative Art of Garnishing

The Creative Art of Garnishing

More than 130 exciting
ideas and easy-to-follow instructions
for decorating food

Yvette Stachowiak

Crescent Books
New York

Published by Salamander Books Ltd
129-137 York Way,
London N7 9LG,
United Kingdom

This 1990 edition published by
Crescent Books, distribution
by Crown Publishers, Inc.,
225 Park Avenue South,
New York, New York 10003.

ISBN 0-517-69412-3
h g f e d c b a

All correspondence concerning the content
of this volume should be addressed to
Salamander Books Ltd.

The publishers would like to thank Rosemary Wadey
for her invaluable help and advice in compiling
this book, particularly for writing the majority
of the chapter on Icings and Decorations.

The publishers would also like to thank Kitchen
Devils for their support and supply of equipment
for photography.

Editors: Gillian Haslam, Barbara Croxford
    and Helen Dore
Art direction: Roger Hyde
Design: Stonecastle Graphics Ltd
Photographer: Barry Chapman
Cookery Consultants and Home Economists:
    Emma Lee Gow and Rosemary Wadey

Typeset by SX Composing Ltd
Colour reproduction by
    Scantrans Pte Ltd, Singapore
Printed and bound in Italy

Contents

Introduction

*A*ttractive presentation makes all the difference to good food. A dish that looks beautiful will taste even better. Garnishing has an important part to play in all food presentation, particularly of course for entertaining. But whether for party or home cooking, a garnish should enhance the appearance of a dish and at the same time complement its taste.

Garnishing is an art in itself, but that does not mean that it has to be elaborate; over-decorated food does not look appetizing, and can be off-putting. Some of the simplest garnishes are the most effective — a fresh lemon and lime twist on a fish steak, for example, or a scattering of bright edible flowers to lend extra colour to a simple green salad. There is much to learn from the Japanese in this respect, who have made a real art of simple yet stunning food garnishes. And some dishes scarcely need any garnishing at all — their ingredients are sufficiently decorative in themselves.

All cooks who take pride in their work will want to add that special professional finishing touch, and that is what this book sets out to provide: a wealth of imaginative garnishing ideas, sweet and savoury, some very simple, others more fanciful, all illustrated with clear, easy-to-follow, step-by-step instructions.

Whatever ingredients you choose for your garnishes, make sure they are absolutely fresh. Herbs, for example, make some of the most naturally attractive garnishes — feathery sprays of dill; dainty chervil sprigs; brilliant green bouquets of deep-fried parsley; glossy bay leaves; frosted mint leaves; a sprinkling of finely snipped chives — but they are best used straight from the garden or window-box. Make sure, too, that the garnish complements the flavour and character of the dish, and remember that colour and texture are all-important. Ideally most garnishes should be added just before serving, so allow yourself a few extra minutes in which to do this.

Essential Equipment

As with any branch of cooking, garnishing can only be as good as the equipment you use. In fact, using the right equipment is essential if you are to achieve the precise cutting and intricate trimming which garnishing often requires. To get the very best results, you need first-class tools — it's a false economy to buy anything cheap as it will rust or lose its sharp cutting edge quickly. On the other hand, there is no point in getting carried away and buying dozens of gadgets. They may seem an inspired purchase at the time, but can all too often end up languishing at the back of a kitchen drawer. The best idea is to select and buy the best you can afford and this chapter will give you all the advice you need on how to build up a really sensible and useful repertoire of special tools. For example, invaluable information on the different kinds of knife available for a variety of tasks, from cutting the petals for a radish rose to chopping the finest of herbs, from grooving a mushroom to slicing a cucumber. Specialist tools, such as the tiny, attractively shaped cutters for stamping out aspic or pastry shapes; a melon baller which can also be used for butter garnishes; and a lemon zester that produces fine lemon shreds, are also described.

Bread knife

Steel

8¼ in (20.5 cm)
carving knife

5¼ in (13 cm)
kitchen knife

4 in (10 cm)
cook's knife

Vegetable knife

——————— Knives ———————

For any culinary work, the first and foremost tool is a good knife. You will have to spend a little more money, but you can rest assured that your purchase will last a long time. Selecting a knife is a very individual matter – take your time to ensure you get one you feel comfortable with.

Your knife handle is almost as important as your blade. Choose a handle that feels comfortable and well balanced. The composition of the material should be rosewood, high-quality plastic or mixed wood and plastic. The handle should also have a full tang (the steel in the handle, visible through the front and back).

There are four types of knife blade available: carbon steel, which is easily corroded but sharpens well; stainless steel, which is very difficult to sharpen but does

not corrode; high carbon stainless steel, which has the advantages of carbon steel and stainless steel but none of the disadvantages; and super stainless steel, which cannot be sharpened.

A knife must be sharp to be of any real use. It is a common misconception that sharp knives are dangerous, in fact dull knives cause accidents as you have to exert more pressure on the knife to slice anything – slippage and subsequent cuts then occur. The most common method of sharpening a knife is to use a sharpening steel. Remember to sharpen the whole length of the blade and not just one section – this becomes easier with practice. Finally, always cut on a wooden chopping board – never use a plastic or laminated surface as both the surface and your knife will be ruined. Really sharp kitchen scissors can often be a good alteration to a knife for fiddly trimming and snipping.

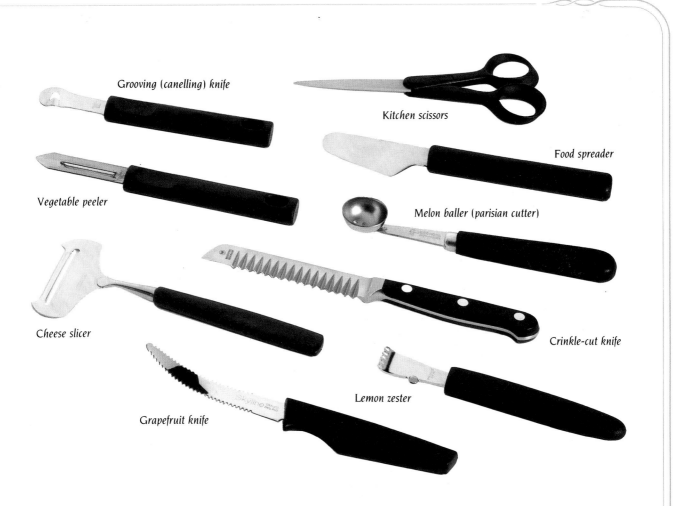

Grooving (canelling) knife

Kitchen scissors

Food spreader

Vegetable peeler

Melon baller (parisian cutter)

Cheese slicer

Crinkle-cut knife

Grapefruit knife

Lemon zester

The two knives indispensable to kitchen work are: a small kitchen knife and a French (cook's) knife with a blade between 20-30cm (8-12in) long. In addition, a palette knife for smoothing and lifting, a carving knife, a grooving (canelling) knife, a crinkle-cut knife, a vegetable peeler, a curved grapefruit knife and a bread knife are among the many other choices available.

Decorative cutters

A collection of small and large decorative cutters is most useful for biscuits and pastry, aspic, chocolate and marzipan work.

Butter shapers

More specialist tools include those for making butter garnishes. A butter cutter combines several functions, including making butter balls, fluted slices and curls. Ribbed wooden butter paddles are used for shaping butter balls, while wooden butter moulds are an easy way of decorating butter slices.

Melon baller (Parisian cutter), grooving (canelling) knife and lemon zester

These are all useful, inexpensive tools to have. The melon baller (Parisian cutter) can also be employed for potato balls, coring halved fruits, hollowing out cherry tomatoes or cucumber slices, and butter balls. The grooving (canelling) knife is not just for citrus fruit, but can also be used for cucumber or mushrooms. The lemon zester, in particular, is the handiest way of removing the outer zest from a lemon, or other citrus fruits leaving the bitter pith behind.

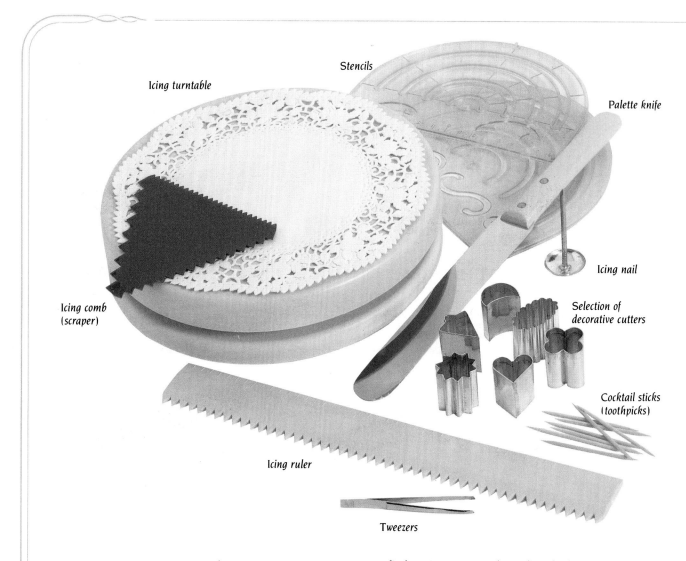

Stencils

Icing turntable

Palette knife

Icing nail

Selection of
decorative cutters

Icing comb
(scraper)

Cocktail sticks
(toothpicks)

Icing ruler

Tweezers

Brushes

Brushes are essential for both pastry and aspic work. There are two colours of brush available – black and white. As a rule of thumb, use a dark brush if you are working with light-coloured foods, and vice versa: a bristle can sometimes come out of the brush, and if the bristle is darker or lighter than the item you are using it on, you can then easily see it and remove it. The two most useful sizes for brushes are those with a bristle width of ⅛in (3mm) and 2in (5cm).

Cake icing equipment

You must collect all the items you need before you start, for icing does not take kindly to being left around whilst

you find a missing item. Always buy the best quality equipment possible and look after it well. Dents in icing nozzles (pipes) and chips out of rulers and combs only add frustration by spoiling hard work. Always wash and dry your equipment scrupulously after use and check it again before using it the next time.

Apart from the usual kitchen equipment which is available such as bowls, basins, measuring spoons, wooden spoons, sieves, spatulas, pastry brushes and kitchen scissors, the following are the basic essentials for an ambitious cake icer.

Icing turntable – make sure it is steady and turns evenly so you can ice your cake perfectly.

Icing ruler – either plastic or metal for levelling the tops of cakes and measuring for designs.

Icing comb or scraper – made in plastic for decorating

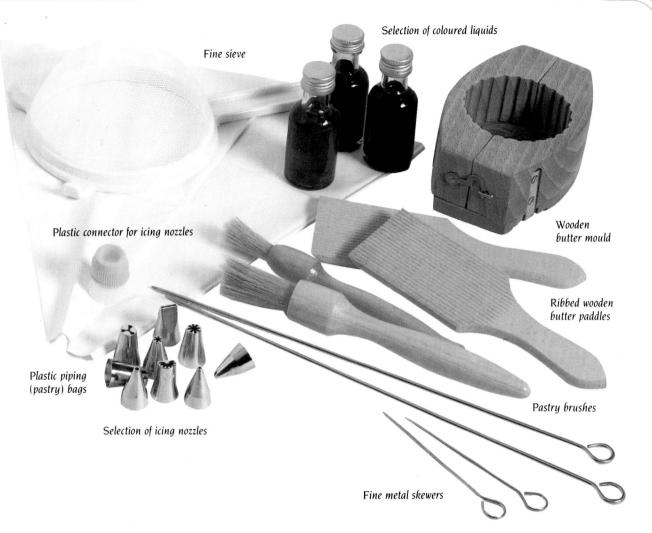

Fine sieve

Selection of coloured liquids

Plastic connector for icing nozzles

Wooden butter mould

Ribbed wooden butter paddles

Plastic piping (pastry) bags

Selection of icing nozzles

Pastry brushes

Fine metal skewers

the sides of cakes. They come both straight edged and serrated to give straight sides and corners and interesting wavy lines to sides and tops of cakes.

Non-stick silicone paper – for making flowers, runouts, collars etc and for marzipan and fondant icing shapes and for rolling out anything that might stick.

Piping (pastry) bags – are made of canvas or plastic (there are also rigid metal 'bags'). If using a canvas bag, make sure to use it with the ragged fabric seam outside. Alternatively, you can make your own icing bag from greaseproof (waxed) paper, as shown on page 140.

Icing nozzles (pipes) – a selection of nozzles (pipes) including fine, medium and thick, writing, petal, various sizes of stars and shells, rosette, ribbon, leaf etc.

Tweezers – for picking up delicate piped icing shapes to attach to cakes.

Selection of coloured pastes and liquids – start with a selection of the basic colours – they can be enlarged on as you progress. Colours can be added to all types of icings to spread, pipe and mould in varying degrees from pastel to very deep shades.

Icing nail – to attach small squares of non-stick silicone paper for piping flowers on. The nail is easily twisted between the fingers to make a perfect flower.

Large and small palette knives or spatulas – essential for spreading icings of all types on to cakes and for many of the simple designs. Also good for mixing colours into icings etc.

Fine skewers and cocktail sticks – essential for lifting off broken and incorrect piping from cakes, for shaping and helping with moulding and rolled out marzipan shapes and for runouts etc.

1
Vegetable Garnishes

W ith such a colourful variety to choose from, vegetables make some of the most attractive garnishes. They can be used for all kinds of savoury dishes, from soups, sandwiches and salads to more elaborate party pieces. It's fun to experiment with the more exotic vegetables such as chillis and aubergines (eggplants) (pages 23 and 28), but with just a little ingenuity, even the commonplace carrot and potato can be made highly decorative. But whichever vegetable you choose, you will only get perfect results if it is even-sized, at just the right degree of ripeness to work with, and totally free of blemishes.

A single tomato rose looks attractive garnishing a slice of pâté or as a centrepiece for an individual green salad or pale savoury mousse, such as avocado or smoked haddock. Groups of roses make the highlight of a vegetable bouquet (*see pages 26 and 27*).

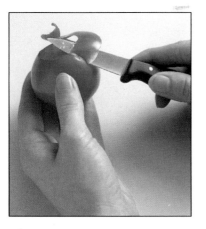

1 Place a firm ripe tomato stalk-side (stem-side) down on a chopping board. Cut a thin base from the tomato with a small sharp knife, leaving it attached to the tomato. Hold the tomato in your hand, stalk-side down. Using the knife in a zigzag motion, cut a thin continuous ¾ in (2 cm) wide spiral of tomato skin, starting from the cut base to the top of the tomato.

2 Lay the strip of skin flesh side down. Start at the bottom end of the strip and roll up completely.

3 To finish the rose, spread the 'petals' gently apart, using your fingers or a cocktail stick (toothpick), to make the rose look more realistic.

Use tomato flowers as part of a colourful crudités assortment to accompany a dip, in salads, or to garnish cold party dishes, such as Italian Vitello Tonnato, sliced veal in a pale pink tuna sauce.

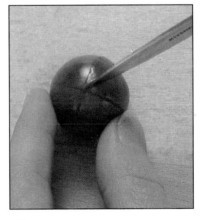

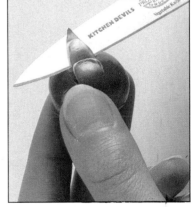

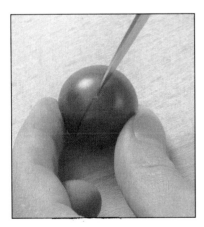

1 Place a small firm cherry tomato stalk-side (stem-side) down on a chopping board. Make a cut, using a small sharp knife, just through the skin of the tomato, starting from the top of the tomato to within ¼ in (5 mm) of the base. Make another cut just through the skin of the tomato, directly opposite the first cut on the top, to within ¼ in (5 mm) of the base.

2 Turn the tomato an eighth of a turn and, starting again at the top, cut just through the skin to run close to the base. Make a matching cut directly opposite. Repeat twice, turning the tomato an eighth of a turn each time.

3 Carefully peel the tomato skin 'petals' away from the tomato flesh with the knife, starting from the top and peeling almost to the base. A small herb sprig, such as parsley or chervil, or a small strip of lemon zest may be inserted in the centre of the tomato.

*R*osy-pink radish flowers, with their contrasting white centres, look attractive on a rice salad or cold meat platter for a buffet meal. To make the petals open, soak the radishes in ice water for 30 minutes.

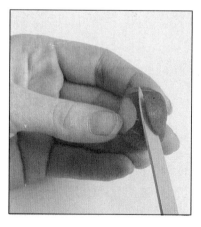

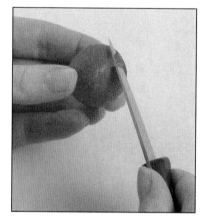

1 For a *radish rose*, carefully trim both ends of a radish. Using a small sharp knife, make 4 curved cuts, each starting from the root end of the radish and following along the length of the radish just to the stalk (stem) end, without cutting through. Each cut should just overlap the previous one.

2 For a *radish bud*, carefully trim both ends of a radish. Make 4 lengthwise and 6 crosswise incisions three-quarters of the way into the root end of the radish. Be careful not to cut all the way through the radish.

3 For a *radish lily*, carefully trim both ends of a radish. Make 12 cuts, each starting from the root end of the radish and following along the length of the radish almost as far down as the stalk (stem). Using the tip of a small sharp knife, detach the 'petals' from the white of the radish by running the knife underneath the petals, but leave the lower ends attached.

Chinese Carrot Flowers

These look pretty as a garnish to an oriental dish: they would look stunning with brilliant green stir-fried mangetout. They also make appetizing and healthy crudités to nibble with aperitifs.

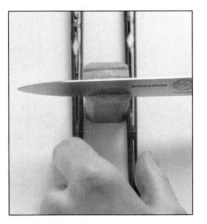

1 Peel a medium carrot, then cut into 1 in (2.5 cm) in rectangles. Round off the corners slightly. Place the rectangle, cut side down, between 2 chopsticks and make 4 cuts horizontally with a small sharp knife, cutting down as far as the chopsticks. (The chopsticks prevent the knife from cutting through to the base of the carrot.)

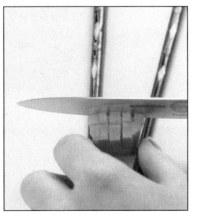

2 Turn the carrot 90° and make 4 vertical cuts. Sprinkle salt into the cuts and leave for 30 minutes.

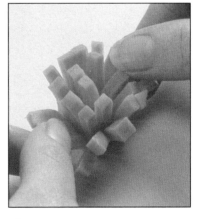

3 Rinse the carrot flower and dry well, then gently open up the cuts with your fingers. Place the flower on diamond-shaped leaves cut from cucumber skin.

Carrot Flowers

Use to garnish vegetable pâtés, especially a layered pâté of parsnip, carrot and spinach. Scatter on simple green salads or float on bowls of pale creamy vegetable soup, such as Vichyssoise, for added interest.

1 Peel a medium carrot, then cut into 2 in (5 cm) lengths. Using a small sharp knife, make a V-shaped incision lengthwise along the carrot, about ¼ in (5 mm) in depth, and remove the strip of carrot.

2 Turn the carrot slightly and make another lengthwise V-shaped incision ¼ in (5 mm) in depth, again removing the strip of carrot.

3 Repeat 3 more times evenly around the carrot. There should be 5 V-shaped incisions on the carrot. Finally, cut the carrot into ¼ in (5 mm) slices. Caviar may be added to make the flower centre, and chives used as stems.

Chilli Flowers

Pungent red or green chilli flowers are ideal garnishes for the spicy dishes of India and South-East Asia. Use them to give a special touch to a simple vegetarian potato and cauliflower curry, Aloo Gobi, or the popular Indonesian rice dish, Nasi Goreng. When de-seeding chillies, always make sure the juice does not come into contact with your hands or eyes, as it is highly pungent.

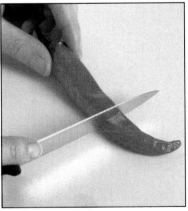

1 Use small green or red chillies for this garnish. Alternatively, trim the pointed end from larger ones and use the stalk (stem) end for the garnish.

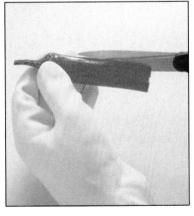

2 Wearing rubber gloves and with a small pair of scissors, slit the chillies lengthwise from the tip end at 8 equal intervals, leaving at least 1 in (2.5 cm) of the stalk end intact.

3 Gently scrape out the seeds and ribs. Stand the chillies in a bowl of ice water for 1 hour or until curled.

As part of a vegetable bouquet (see pages 26 and 27) or as a garnish to a platter of cold meats such as rare beef or pastrami, courgette (zucchini) asters are a simple and effective addition.

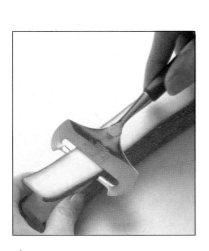

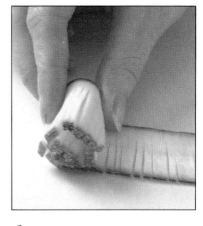

1 Trim both ends from a medium courgette (zucchini). Using a mandolin, cheese slicer or vegetable peeler, cut a very thin lengthwise slice from the courgette. Reserve the remainder for another use.

2 Using a small sharp knife, make cuts along one edge of the courgette slice, keeping the cuts close together but taking care not to cut all the way through. The courgette slice should resemble a comb.

3 Gently roll up the slice of courgette and secure at the base with a piece of cocktail stick (toothpick). Stand upright for the 'petals' to open. A small parsley sprig, a finely cut red pepper strip, a pimento-stuffed olive or a small carrot flower (see page 22) may be added as the centre of the aster.

Turnip Chrysanthemums

Turnip chrysanthemums are popular in Japan, where the special criss-cross style of cutting used to make them is called the 'chrysanthemum cut'. Sometimes the Japanese dye the turnips pink with red food colouring and add real chrysanthemum leaves as a special finishing touch. These turnip chrysanthemums would look especially good as a garnish for a tempting tray of assorted Japanese Sushi.

1 Peel a medium, round white turnip. Place on a chopping board with a wooden chopstick on each side of the turnip. Using a medium, sharp knife, make 8-10 slices along the turnip, all the way down to the chopsticks.

2 Turn the turnip 90°, leaving the chopsticks in the same position, and slice the turnip again criss-cross style. Make sure the knife cuts straight and not at an angle.

3 Soak the cut turnip in a mixture of 1 tablespoon salt and 2 cups (16 fl oz/ 450 ml) water to soften for 1-3 hours until the turnip opens up. Gently push the 'petals' from the centre to the outside of the turnip to achieve a realistic appearance.

Vegetable Bouquets

Make a special buffet centrepiece, such as a glazed ham or poached salmon, look even more sensational with these exquisitely arranged vegetable bouquets, in a coat of shimmering aspic. The flowers and leaves for the bouquets can be varied endlessly by using different vegetables and herbs.

1 The flower tops for a vegetable bouquet can be chosen from tomato roses (see page 18), radish flowers (see page 20), etc. If the bouquet is to be placed on a rounded or tilted surface, for example on the side of a whole ham or fish, use flat flowers and leaves. To anchor flowers and leaves on the food, carefully pierce them with a cocktail stick (toothpick), then dip in aspic (see page 52). When all have been positioned, coat with a thin layer of aspic.

2 For very simple stalks (stems) and leaves for your flowers, cut a long strip of cucumber skin. Cut leaves diagonally across the strip.

3 For smaller leaves, cut diamonds from strips of leek and arrange around the stalks.

4 Different leaf shapes can be created by using continental (flat leaf) parsley, chervil sprigs, bay leaves or other fresh herbs.

5 For the flower petals, use small pieces of tomato, thin ovals of courgette (zucchini) or peppers, or diamonds of aubergine (eggplant) skin. Try small cutters to stamp out different shapes. For the heart of the flower, use the yolk of a hard-boiled (hard-cooked) egg or a thin round slice of black olive.

6 For a more extravagant garnish, a thinly sliced truffle can be used, cut into pattern pieces such as diamonds, circles or crescents. These pieces can then be creatively assembled to form any number of designs. An inexpensive replacement for truffles are thinly sliced pieces of stoned (pitted) black olives.

Eggplant Crowns

Aubergines (eggplants) are a very popular vegetable in Mediterranean and Middle Eastern cooking, and these crowns would make an appropriate and attractive garnish for a platter of Mezze, the delicious appetizers served in the Middle East with a glass of ouzo. Aubergine crowns would also be good with the garlicky aubergine dip known in the Middle East as Poor Man's Caviar.

1 Using a small sharp knife, cut a 3 in (7.5 cm) even piece from a baby aubergine (eggplant), then cut the top two-thirds portion of the aubergine into 5 equal sections. Do not cut through to the bottom of the aubergine.

2 Cut a small V-shaped groove in the center of each of the 5 sections. The grooves should extend from the edge to the centre of each section.

3 Carve 5 more V-shaped grooves in the centre of each of the 5 initial cuts. These grooves should extend halfway down the aubergine. Neaten the centre of the aubergine using a small sharp knife. Soak the garnish in ice water until ready to use. Decorate the crown with shapes cut from peppers.

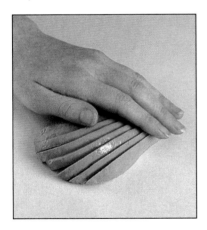

Avocados are very simple to prepare. The only watchpoint is that they should be at just the right degree of ripeness when eaten – not too hard and not too soft. To prepare an avocado, halve, remove the stone (pit), then peel the avocado with a small sharp knife. Immediately rub the avocado flesh with a small amount of lemon juice to prevent discoloration. Serve avocado fans, with a vinaigrette made with raspberry vinegar as an accompaniment for grilled (broiled) or poached fish.

1 For an avocado fan, halve, stone (pit) and peel an avocado. Trim off a small slice at the stalk (stem) end with a small sharp knife. Starting at the wider end of the avocado, make 5 or 7 lengthwise cuts almost to the stalk end. Press gently on the avocado with your hand, so that the slices 'fan' out.

2 For a horizontally fanned avocado, halve, stone (pit) and peel an avocado. Trim off a small slice at the stalk end with a small sharp knife. Place the peeled avocado half, cut side down, on a palette knife (or metal spatula). Make 12 horizontal, evenly spaced cuts through the avocado with a small sharp knife.

3 Slide the slices directly on to a plate with the help of the palette knife. Press gently on the avocado with your hand to fan out the slices.

Vegetable Bundles

*H*ot vegetable bundles are particularly attractive as a garnish for grilled (broiled) meats or fish. Presented cold, they are a delightfully different way of serving crudités. Use a selection of vegetables, choosing from cooked potatoes, cooked Jerusalem artichokes; or cooked or raw carrots, turnips, parsnips, celeriac, swedes (rutabagas), courgettes (zucchini), cucumbers, squashes, peppers, celery, fennel and bamboo shoots.

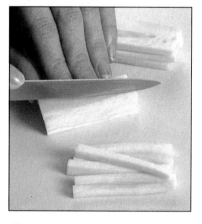

1 For *julienne vegetables*, trim the rounded edges from a 2 in (5 cm) piece of vegetable so it is rectangular in shape. Using a small sharp knife, cut the vegetable lengthwise into ⅛ in (3 mm) slices, making thin 'sheets'. Cut the sheets lengthwise into ⅛ in (3 mm) matchsticks.

2 For *bâton vegetables*, trim the rounded edges from a 2½ in (6 cm) piece of vegetable so it is rectangular in shape. Using a small sharp knife, cut the vegetables lengthwise into ¼ in (5 mm) slices. Cut the slices lengthwise into ¼ in (5 mm) pieces.

3 For *green vegetable ties*, pour boiling water over the green part of a spring onion (scallion) or leek to soften. Drain and rinse under cold water, then pat dry. Cut the spring onion or leek into long narrow strips, then use to tie a bundle of vegetables. For *orange vegetable ties*, blanch thin strips of carrot until pliable. Small blanched white or red onion rings may also be used to hold vegetable bundles together.

Celery Curls

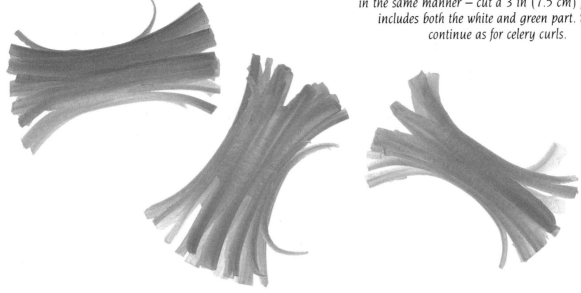

Celery curls look fun on crudité platters or in salads. They are especially good with cheese: use them to garnish a whole Stilton, a cheeseboard or individual cheese plates. Spring onions (scallions) can be trimmed in the same manner — cut a 3 in (7.5 cm) piece which includes both the white and green part. Simply continue as for celery curls.

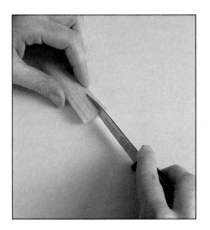

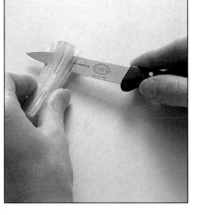

1 Cut a piece of celery stick 2 in (5 cm) in length. Using a small sharp knife, cut down into the lengthwise grain of each strip as many times as you can, in about a third towards the centre.

2 Repeat at the other end of the stick, again making as many tiny cuts as possible, in about a third towards the centre. Turn the celery piece 90° and cut widthwise through the tiny cuts on both ends, down a third towards the centre.

3 Soak in a bowl of ice water for about 1 hour to allow the celery to curl.

This is one vegetable dish that people cannot resist – the unusual shape and fresh flavour of these courgettes (zucchini) make them an admirable accompaniment for main dishes with sauces, and they are easy to prepare and cook.

Ingredients

SERVES 4

2 tablespoons freshly grated Parmesan cheese

1 tablespoon fresh white breadcrumbs

6 tablespoons (3 oz/75 g) unsalted (sweet) butter, softened

2 tablespoons finely chopped fresh parsley

1½ teaspoons finely chopped fresh tarragon leaves or ½ teaspoon dried tarragon

salt and freshly ground black pepper, to taste

4 courgettes (zucchini), each 6 in (15 cm) in length

1 Preheat the oven to 400F (200C/Gas 6). Combine the Parmesan cheese and breadcrumbs in a small bowl and set aside. In another bowl, thoroughly mix the remaining ingredients, except for the courgettes (zucchini).

2 Keeping the stalk (stem) end attached, cut each courgette lengthwise into four or five ½ in (1 cm) thick slices. Spread some of the herb butter carefully between the layers and press the slices together lightly. Separate the slices slightly to form a fan, then place in a buttered 15½×10½×1 in (38×25×2.5 cm) flameproof dish. Cook in the oven for 20 minutes or until just tender.

3 Sprinkle the fans with the breadcrumb mixture and grill (broil) under a preheated grill about 4 in (10 cm) from the heat for 1-2 minutes or until golden.

Crinkle-cut Vegetables

*R*ing the changes for crudités by crinkle-cutting the vegetables with a serrated knife. This technique is also good to give a new twist to cooked vegetable dishes. Most firm vegetables, such as carrots, cucumber, courgettes (zucchini), beetroot (beet), mushrooms or peppers can be crinkle-cut.

1 For *crinkle-cut circles or slices*, peel and trim the vegetable where appropriate, then, using a small serrated knife, simply cut through the vegetable to the required thickness.

2 For *crinkle-cut sticks*, peel and trim the vegetable where appropriate, then, using the serrated knife, cut into slices 2½×½ in (6×1 cm) thick. Turn the slices 90°, then cut the slices into ½ in (1 cm) sticks. Potatoes so cut can make deep-fried chips (French fries).

3 Savoury items, such as hard-boiled (hard-cooked) eggs or hard cheese can be trimmed with a serrated knife, and so can firm fruits. Butter wedges can also be cut with a serrated knife for a simple yet effective presentation.

Give an elegant finishing touch to fish with these pretty fans. Their cool green colour would enhance a dinner party dish of sole or scallops.

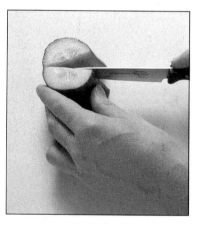

1 Cut a cucumber piece 1½ in (4 cm) long on the diagonal. Cut the piece in half lengthwise.

2 Cut thin slices at the same angle, taking care not to cut all the way through. Make 9 cuts in the piece of cucumber.

3 Turn the cucumber over and bend back every other slice to the joined end, leaving the alternate slices straight. Leave in a bowl of ice water for several hours before using.

Cucumber Crowns

Cucumber crowns can be used to garnish cold chicken or fish dishes, or simply served as crudités. As a garnish, they look most attractive, as well as providing a sauce, if filled as suggested in step 3. Red caviar or lumpfish roe could be spooned on top of the cream sauce, and the crowns could also be filled with a smooth vegetable purée. For cocktail snacks, pipe a creamy blue cheese or pâté mixture into the scooped out crowns.

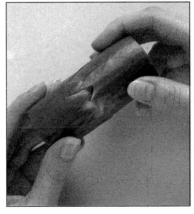

1 Cut an unpeeled cucumber into 3½-4 in (9-10 cm) lengths. Make continuous V-shaped cuts into the centre all around the middle of the cucumber.

2 Gently twist the halves apart. Garnish the centre of each crown with sprigs of fresh herbs or small circles of red pepper.

3 Alternatively, carefully scoop out the centre with the handle of a teaspoon and fill with a savoury cream sauce such as soured cream and chives or paprika.

Cucumber Spirals

*C*ucumber spirals are fun for children's parties or as a garnish for meat platters. Choose small cucumbers with few seeds.

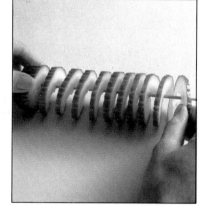

1 Cut the cucumber into 3 in (7.5 cm) pieces, discarding the ends. Push a wooden skewer (or chopstick) through the centre of the cucumber.

2 Holding a small sharp knife at an angle in one hand and the cucumber in the other, cut through to the centre of the cucumber until the knife touches the skewer. Continue cutting around the cucumber, turning the cucumber as you cut until the end is reached.

3 Remove the skewer and pull the end of the cucumber so it forms a 'spiral'. A circle can be made by hooking the two ends of the 'spring' together.

Turned Mushrooms

Turned mushrooms usually decorate fish dishes or garnish colourful mixed salads. Grooved mushrooms, a simpler version of turned mushrooms, are made using a canelle (grooving) knife.

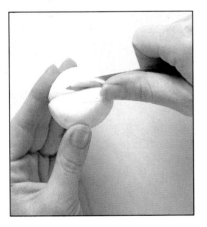

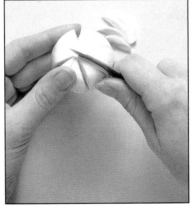

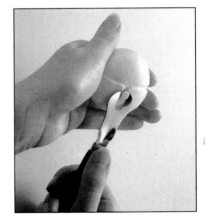

1 Hold the blade of a small sharp knife loosely in your fingers at a slight angle, the cutting edge balanced on the mushroom. Place the side of your thumb behind the blade, on the top of the mushroom.

2 Using your thumb as a pivot, push the blade foward and down in a smooth motion by twisting your wrist. The slanted cutting edge should carve a strip out of the mushroom cap. Continue carving strips at regular intervals while turning the mushroom until the first strip is reached. Cut off and discard the stalk (stem) or save for soups, stocks etc.

3 To make *grooved mushrooms*, starting from the centre of the mushroom cap, draw the knife downwards to the stalk (stem). Turn the mushroom slightly and continue drawing 7 more grooves, each evenly spaced around the mushroom.

Use these leek leaves to provide foliage for the vegetable bouquets on pages 26 and 27. Blanching the leek strips before cutting makes them more pliable and retains their vivid green colour.

1 Using a single long green strip of blanched leek and a small sharp knife, cut the strip into rectangular pieces between 1-3 in (2.5-7.5 cm), depending on the size of leaf required.

2 Make a curved cut from the top left hand corner of the strip to the bottom right hand corner.

3 To finish, turn the leaf 180° and make another curved cut to match the first.

Two-colour Leek Leaves

These are ideal to include as part of a decorative design for dishes coated in aspic, such as Chaudfroid of chicken, cold salmon, or a savoury jellied salad.

1 Blanch strips of leek in boiling water, making sure you use both the green and white parts of the leek. Using a small sharp knife, cut the strips into rectangular pieces between 2-3 in (5-7.5 cm), depending on the size of leaf required.

2 Take a green rectangle of leek. Using pinking shears, cut a curve from the top right hand corner towards the centre of the rectangle then curve the cut back towards the bottom right hand corner at the end of the cut.

3 The 'leaf' should have one straight side and one pinked curved side. Repeat with a white rectangle of leek. To assemble the leaf, place the straight sides of one green portion and one white portion together.

These are perfect in salads, or for accompanying a savoury dip. Use green, red and yellow peppers, and, if you can obtain them, the exciting black ones available from food stores specializing in exotic fruit and vegetables.

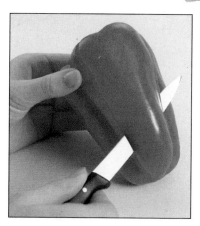  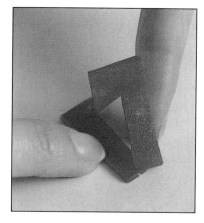

1 Cut a flat piece from a pepper, and trim to a rectangle about 1×¾ in (2.5×2 cm) with a small sharp knife. Cut off the fleshy underside and remove the ribs and seeds.

2 Make a cut along the long edge of the rectangle, about one third of the way in, leaving one end attached. Make a second cut parallel to the first, taking care not to cut all the way through.

3 Hold the 2 ends of the pepper and twist to make a triangle. The triangle will hold its shape when the 2 ends butt up against each other.

*C*lever cutting can transform the humble potato into a full-blown rose! Potato roses make an attractive addition to a vegetable bouquet (*see pages 26 and 27*), used to garnish cold meat or fish platters. Turnips or large carrots can be treated in the same manner or used as an individual garnish.

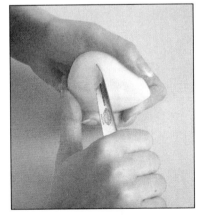

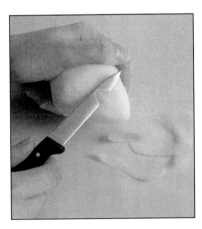

1 Using a small sharp knife, cut a pointed cone-shape from the top of a peeled potato. Trim the bottom third of the potato to make it look like a child's toy top.

2 To begin the petals, make a row of curved downward slits, approximately ¾ in (2 cm) long, around the widest part of the potato, making sure not to cut more than one third into the potato. Using the tip of the knife, trim off a ¼-½ in (5 mm-1 cm) strip of potato above the row of slits, following the widest point of the potato. Pull out the strip of potato to expose the bottom layer of petals.

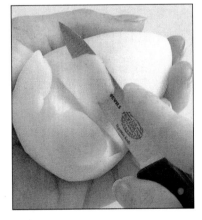

3 Keep cutting layers of slits, alternating the position of the petals to create a true flower effect. Cut off the top of the rose to level it with the last layer of petals. Carve out petal shapes in the centre of the rose to make it more lifelike. Blanch the rose for 1 minute in boiling water, then cool in cold water to prevent discoloration.

Duchess Potatoes

*D*uchess potatoes are simply mashed potatoes enriched by the addition of egg, then piped into a variety of shapes and baked until attractively browned and crisp. They are perfect for grilled (broiled) and roasted meats or as a garnish for casseroles. The success of these potatoes depends on a lump-free potato purée. If, after puréeing or mashing the potatoes, there are still lumps, push them through a medium sieve to obtain the finest texture.

Ingredients

4 cups (1 lb/450 g) hot puréed or very finely mashed potatoes
4 tablespoons (2 oz/50 g) unsalted (sweet) butter
pinch of freshly grated nutmeg
salt and freshly ground white pepper
1 egg
2 egg yolks
butter, for greasing
beaten egg, for glazing

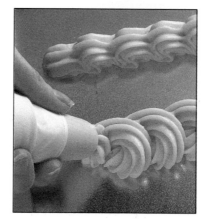

1 Place the potatoes in a saucepan over a medium heat and stir with a wooden spoon to evaporate all the moisture. When the purée is dry, remove the pan from the heat and add the butter and seasonings. Stirring vigorously, add the egg and egg yolks. Butter a glass or enamel dish, then fill with the purée. Place a small piece of butter on a fork and rub over the top to prevent a skin from forming. Allow to cool.

2 Pipe the duchess potatoes in long ropes or twisted ropes as a decorative border to meat or fish dishes, using the method shown above. Finish off in the oven as described in step 3.

3 Alternatively, pipe into stars or rosettes, or into nests which can be filled with various vegetables or meat mixtures. Brush with beaten egg and brown in an oven preheated to 400F (200C/Gas 6).

These potatoes are a traditional garnish for roast and grilled (broiled) meats. Carrots, turnips, parsnips and courgettes (zucchini) may be prepared in the same shape. These are normally braised (cooked slowly with a little stock, butter and flavouring ingredients), rather than fried; the addition of sugar or honey to the butter and oil mixture towards the end of cooking will give the vegetables a shiny, appetizing glaze.

1 Cut a large potato in half widthwise. Cut each half into 2 pieces. Cut the quarters into equal elongated pieces.

2 Trim or 'turn' each piece to make a little barrel-shaped potato. Do not trim the ends of the potato pieces into points or they will burn while cooking – keep the ends flat.

3 Blanch the potatoes in boiling water for 1 minute, then drain well and pat dry with kitchen paper towels. To finish, fry in a mixture of butter and oil until browned and tender.

These tomatoes are generally stuffed with a savoury mixture based on ham, eggs or chicken, or salad such as rice or potato. They are particularly attractive as part of a buffet. Use good-sized, firm tomatoes with their stalks (stems) still attached, or smaller tomatoes to serve as cocktail canapés.

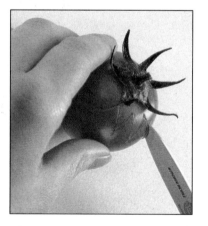

1 Using a small sharp knife, make continuous zigzag cuts just near the top of the stalk (stem) end of the tomato. The cuts should be equal in size and go halfway into the tomato.

2 Pull the cap away from the rest of the tomato by holding the tomato in both hands and easing apart.

3 Using a small spoon, scoop out the flesh and seeds from the tomato. Pat the inside dry with kitchen paper towels, then generously fill with your favourite stuffing. Replace the cap at an angle, balancing it on the filling.

Tomato Starbursts

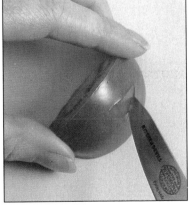

The tomato starburst can be used in 3 ways: all the wedges can be reassembled to make the original shape; a single wedge may be laid flat, or a pair of wedges laid pointing towards each other. Use the complete tomato starburst as a stunning centre-point for a simple summer salad of sliced cucumber and watercress sprigs.

1 Cut off a thin slice from the stalk (stem) end of the tomato, using a small sharp knife. Turn the tomato cut side down, then cut the tomato into 6 equal wedges.

2 In the centre of the skin side of each tomato wedge, make 2 cuts, 1/8 in (3 mm) deep, to form a V-shape. The point of the V should face the narrow end of the tomato wedge.

3 Separate the skin from the tomato by starting at the pointed end and continue cutting to two-thirds of the length of the tomato wedge. Gently bend back the skin from the rest of the wedge to form a petal. Repeat the process on remaining tomato wedges.

*B*utterfly tomatoes give an unusual and sophisticated finish to a party salad, arranged in a border so they look as though they are flying round the edge of the bowl.

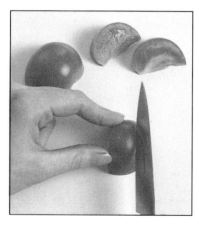

1 Cut a firm ripe tomato into 8 even-sized wedges.

2 Using a small sharp knife, peel the skin away from the flesh of the wedge, starting at the pointed end. Cut halfway down the wedge, leaving the remainder of the skin attached to the tomato.

3 Gently bend back the skin of each tomato wedge. Place 2 wedges, skin-side together, and position them to resemble a butterfly.

Radish Fans and Spinners

*R*adish fans and spinners are frequently used for crudités or as a garnish for salads, sandwiches or cold platters. They are ideal for party food, as they can be made several hours in advance and left in a bowl of ice water in the refrigerator. Other vegetables which can be cut as fans include courgettes (zucchini), cucumbers, baby aubergines (eggplants) and pickled gherkins.

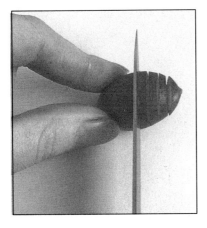

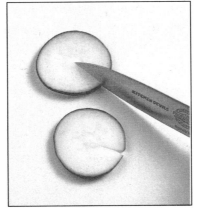

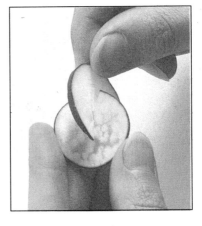

1 To make *fans*, using an oval-shaped radish, carefully trim off the root and stalk (stem) ends with a small sharp knife. Make crosswise cuts along the radish, taking care not to slice all the way through. Place in a bowl of ice water and leave to soak for several hours until the fan opens up.

2 To make *spinners*, carefully trim off the root and stalk (stem) ends from a radish. Cut the radish thinly in crosswise slices. Using a small sharp knife, make a notch in each slice, cutting from the centre to the outside.

3 Holding 1 slice of radish in each hand, gently push 1 slice into the other at the notch so they connect to form a spinner. Repeat with the remaining radish slices. Small cucumber slices can be used in the same manner.

Spring Onion Tassels

Use fresh, plump spring onions for the best effect. Have a bowl of ice water ready to put them in as soon as they are cut. Use to garnish steaks, chops, salads, cold meats, etc. and particularly any Chinese dishes.

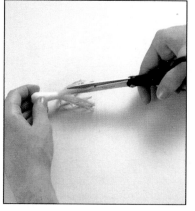

1 Trim the onion to a 2-3 in (5-7.5 cm) length, strip off outer leaves and cut off the root.

2 Take a pair of kitchen scissors and make cuts into the stem of the onion to within 1 in (2.5 cm) of the base, keeping them as close as possible.

3 Put immediately into a bowl of ice water and place in the refrigerator for 1-2 hours until they open out and curl into tassels. Drain well before serving.

This combination of red and green looks pretty on cold poached white fish, or on pâtés. To anchor the garnish firmly, carefully coat with aspic (see page 52) and allow to set.

1 Using a small sharp knife, cut a red pepper into neat ¾ in (2 cm) strips. Trim away most of the fleshy underside and remove the ribs and seeds. Blanch the pepper strips in a saucepan of boiling water for 30 seconds, then immediately plunge them into cold water. Cut the pepper neatly into ¾ in (2 cm) diamonds.

2 Using a potato peeler, remove the skin from a cucumber in long ¾ in (2 cm) wide strips. Blanch the cucumber skin in a saucepan of boiling water for 30 seconds, then plunge it immediately into cold water. Cut the cucumber skin neatly into ¾ in (2 cm) diamonds.

3 Using a cocktail stick (toothpick), dip the pepper and cucumber diamonds one by one into aspic jelly, then arrange on the food to be garnished. Leaving spaces between the pepper and cucumber allows the colour of the food being garnished to show through. Refrigerate. When the aspic has set, spoon another very thin layer of aspic jelly over the food and allow to set once again.

Savoury Garnishes

In this section you will find some interesting ideas for transforming everyday ingredients such as butter, eggs and cheese into really special garnishes. Pretty creamy-yellow butter roses will delight and intrigue dinner guests; pats of savoury butters will lend a superb finishing touch to both the flavour and appearance of plain grilled steaks or cutlets; tiny herb-coated mixed cheese balls, or eggs stuffed with a variety of tasty fillings will prove irresistible on salads. There are also full instructions on how to make and use aspic, giving you all the know-how you need to create some of the most sophisticated garnishes. Artistic prawn and lobster butterflies will add extra elegance to seafood dishes, and there are handy tips on decorating a variety of sauces and soups.

Aspic

True aspic is made from calves' feet, but the term is used to describe any savoury gelatinous liquid which gels and sets when cold; for cooks in a hurry, aspic powder can be a real boon. Aspic can be flavoured and used in a number of ways: as a binding agent, as a glaze for cold dishes, or in the filling of raised pies. Shapes cut from a thin layer of aspic are popular as a garnish for cold savoury dishes: a set of special aspic cutters will give an especially professional result. The stock used should complement the food to be coated with aspic. For example, use chicken stock for garnishing a chicken, fish stock for coating fish, etc.

Ingredients

MAKES 4½ cups (1¾ pints/1 litre)
5 cups (2 pints/1⅓ litres) good clear fat-free
   stock
2 egg whites
1 cup (3 oz/75 g) leafy part of celery
½ cup (2 oz/50 g) carrots, coarsely chopped
handful of coarsely chopped fresh parsley
1-2 branches coarsely chopped fresh tarragon
½ teaspoon crushed black pepper
salt, to taste
3 sachets unflavoured gelatine

1 Combine all the ingredients except the gelatine together in a large clean saucepan. Bring to the boil over high heat. Stirring occasionally with a clean wooden spoon, boil fast for 4-5 seconds, then remove to the side of the cooker. Dissolve the gelatine in a little water, without boiling, then stir into the saucepan. Leave the mixture to stand for 10 minutes.

2 Strain through a clean fine sieve lined with kitchen paper towels.

3 Variations: Add ¼ cup (2 fl oz/50 ml) Madeira to beef-based stock as a complement to meat dishes. For a fish-based aspic, use fish stock flavoured with a bunch of finely chopped fresh dill, added after straining.

Make sure all your tools and utensils, such as whisks, bowls and saucepans, are super-clean, to prevent the aspic becoming cloudy.

1 To coat food with aspic, have the aspic at approximately 93F (34C). It should be syrupy – about the consistency of unbeaten egg whites. If the aspic is too firm, melt it in a clean metal bowl in a bain-marie. Transfer the bowl to a larger bowl filled with ice cubes and stir occasionally with a clean wooden spoon or whisk, until it is the right temperature. Aspic can be remelted and set a number of times, if handled gently.

2 Place the food to be coated on a metal rack over a clean metal tray. For larger items, carefully pour the aspic over with a small ladle. The excess will drain away (you can spoon it up and use again by remelting), leaving a thin coating.

3 Apply aspic to smaller foods using a small, soft brush. Refrigerate the aspic-coated food to allow the coating to gel. Repeat the process 2-3 times, remelting and setting the aspic as necessary so the food is well coated.

Lining a flat dish with aspic provides a firm base to hold food steady and makes it easier to carry to the table and to carve. For jellied moulds, an aspic lining facilitates turning out, and if appropriately garnished with herbs, decorative slices of vegetables or fruit, etc., gives the mould an attractive and professional finish.

1 To coat a flat-rimmed serving dish with aspic (used frequently as a base for aspic-glazed meat, poultry or fish), pour ¼ in (5 mm) aspic over the base of the dish, using a ladle, and making sure the dish is level. If any bubbles form, remove them by piercing with a cocktail stick (toothpick). Once the dish is coated with aspic, do not touch it again until completely set.

2 To coat a mould with aspic, pour approximately 1 cup (8 fl oz/250 ml) aspic into the wetted mould. Immediately roll it in a larger bowl filled with ice so the aspic coats the side of the mould as it sets. Add more aspic and keep twisting the mould to thicken the coating all over the inside of the mould. The coating should be approximately ¼ in (5 mm) thick.

3 To garnish the mould, place the chosen garnishes attractively inside the mould, both on the base and up the sides. Add a little more aspic, making sure all the items are coated, then leave to set in the refrigerator. Proceed to fill the mould with your chosen filling.

Cutting Out Aspic

*A*spic shapes, stamped out with special cutters or simply cut with a sharp knife, are among the easiest and most effective of all garnishes. Individual aspic shapes look good gleaming on single servings of chicken breast or fish fillet; use chopped aspic to create a shimmering ring around a handsome salmon or cold turkey for a buffet.

1 To cut out aspic shapes or to make chopped aspic, pour aspic on to a clean tray to the required thickness. Transfer to a refrigerator to firm.

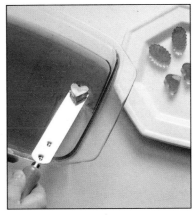

2 Use clean fancy cutters to cut out the aspic shapes. Press the cutter firmly into the aspic, then, with a clean palette knife (or metal spatula) carefully remove the shape. To cut out small squares, rectangles or diamonds, use a ruler balanced on the lip of the tray and run a knife along the ruler into the aspic to make a straight line. Repeat for the required number of shapes.

3 Aspic trimmings can be chopped with a large clean knife to provide a quick decorative edging for a dish. Cut the aspic into slices, then strips. Finally, cut the strips into dice. By twisting the knife left to right while cutting the aspic, you can make 'ridges' on the sides of the slices and dice, giving more glitter to the aspic.

*B*acon curls are the traditional garnish for roast or fried chicken and turkey. They can also be tossed in spinach or cos (romaine) lettuce-based salads, and included in kebabs. Bacon corkscrews make an interesting addition to scrambled or poached eggs on English muffins or North American pancakes, perfect food for brunch.

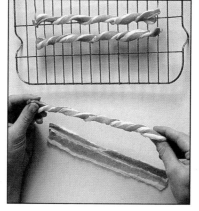

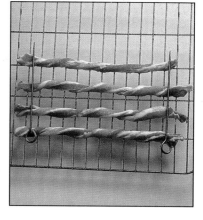

1 For *bacon curls*, cut a rasher (slice) of rindless streaky bacon into 2 or 3 even pieces. Roll up each bacon curl and thread on to a skewer. Place in a shallow dish and cook in a preheated 400F (200C/Gas 6) oven until golden and crisp. Alternatively, the bacon curls may be grilled (broiled), turning frequently to colour evenly. Remove skewers from the bacon and serve hot.

2 For *bacon corkscrews*, run the blunt edge of a knife along rashers (slices) of rindless streaky bacon to stretch them. Twist the slices into spirals and arrange in rows on a wire rack in an ovenproof dish.

3 Put metal skewers across the ends of the bacon rows so that the spirals do not untwist while cooking. Cook in a preheated 375F (190C/Gas 5) oven for 20 minutes or until crisp. Drain the corkscrews on kitchen paper towels.

A special butter cutter – a 3-in-1 tool – combines the making of decorative butter balls, serrated slices or curls. But a melon baller can be used instead for the butter balls and a serrated knife will substitute well for the butter cutter. Only for the butter curls do you need a specialized curler. Keep a chilled block of butter at room temperature for 30 minutes to obtain the right consistency for perfect results. These decorative butters add a very special touch to the dining table.

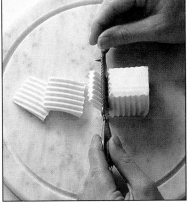

1 For serrated *butter slices*, dip the central portion of the butter cutter into boiling hot water, then immediately cut a slice off a block of semi-hard butter, using the larger ribbed side of the cutter. Both sides will be ridged. Repeat for the required number of slices. If using a serrated knife, dip the knife into boiling hot water after each slice. You can vary the form of the serrated slices by using a triangular or square block of butter.

2 For *butter balls*, dip the rounded portion of the butter cutter into boiling hot water, then press into the butter and turn it smoothly while pressing. Place the balls in a bowl of ice water.

3 If liked, roll the butter balls between 2 wetted ribbed wooden butter paddles before placing them in the ice water so that they have a criss-cross surface. Before serving, butter balls can also be patted dry with kitchen paper towels, then rolled in paprika, crushed black peppercorns or finely chopped fresh parsley.

This is a very decorative way to serve butter. After a little practice, these roses are quite quick to make and can be made well in advance and kept chilled.

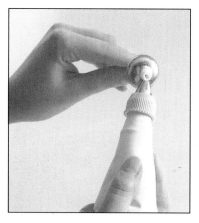

1 Cream room temperature butter with a hand-held electric mixer or wooden spoon for 2 minutes. Fill a piping (pastry) bag fitted with a petal nozzle (tube) half full with the butter.

2 Pipe the butter on to an icing pin while rotating it carefully until a small centre bud is formed.

3 Pipe on eleven to thirteen 1½ in (4 cm) petals, starting from the bud, gently swinging the piping nozzle (tube) upwards for each petal. As you pipe the outer petals, make them wider and longer than the inner petals for a realistic effect. When the rose is finished, gently open out the petals. Place the roses in the refrigerator to harden until needed.

Butter Curls, Crocks and Moulds

Not only do butter curls look decorative, but they are also just the right shape and texture to spread easily. Guests will welcome an individual crock of butter placed at every setting at the table, and will be impressed by professional-looking moulded butter pats.

1 Stand a 1 cup (8oz/225 g) block of firm butter on one of its long sides. Draw a butter curler smoothly along the top long side from end to end (you can either use the top end of a butter cutter, which looks like a ridged bottle opener, or an individual butter curler). Drop the curls into ice water and store in the refrigerator until ready to use.

2 Softened butter or butter trimmings can be placed in small ceramic crocks or pots. Simply level the top or draw wavy lines for an attractive finish. Garnish with a herb sprig or edible flower, such as striking blue borage.

3 You can also use softened butter or butter trimmings for moulded butter. Soak a wooden mould in cold water for a few minutes before using. Press the butter into the mould, then push down the rammer to force out a butter pat stamped with the motif of the mould.

The following butters can be served directly from a ceramic crock or rolled into a sausage shape, then chilled, and sliced as required. Horseradish, mixed chopped fines herbes, and finely grated lemon zest are also good flavourings for savoury butters. These also freeze well.

Lime-Coriander Butter	Nasturtium Butter	Anchovy Butter

Ingredients

MAKES 1 cup (8 oz/225 g)
1 cup (8 oz/225 g) unsalted (sweet) butter, softened
small handful of finely chopped fresh coriander
2 tablespoons fresh lime juice
1 teaspoon grated lime zest
salt, to taste

Ingredients

MAKES approximately 6 tablespoons (3 oz/ 75 g)
5 tablespoons (2½ oz/65 g) unsalted (sweet) butter, softened
1 shallot, finely chopped (minced)
⅛ teaspoon Tabasco hot pepper sauce
small handful nasturtium leaves and blossoms or watercress, shredded

Ingredients

MAKES ½ cup (4 oz/100 g)
½ cup (4 oz/100 g) butter, softened
4 anchovy fillets, rinsed, dried and mashed
1 garlic clove, crushed (minced)
¼ teaspoon lemon juice

1 In a medium bowl, combine all the ingredients. Beat together with a wooden spoon until well blended. Divide the mixture in half. Using 2 sheets of clingfilm (plastic wrap), shape the butter into two 8 in (20 cm) logs; wrap tightly and refrigerate until chilled and firm. The butter can be refrigerated for up to 3 days or frozen for up to 2 months. Use to top hot corn on the cob, grilled (broiled) fish, chicken and steak.

1 Cream the butter until light in a medium bowl. Stir in the remaining ingredients. Cover and refrigerate for up to 4 days. Leave to stand at room temperature for at least 30 minutes before serving. Shredded watercress may be substituted for nasturtium. Try this unusual butter on grilled (broiled) firm white fish.

1 Cream the butter until light in a medium bowl. Blend in the remaining ingredients. Leave to stand at room temperature for 30 minutes before serving. Serve with grilled (broiled) fish or steak.

An easy professional-looking garnish for cutlets, chicken legs and ham on the bone. Use stiff white paper or thick white greaseproof (waxed) or non-stick silicone paper. For parties, make quantities of paper frills in advance, ready for use.

1 Take a piece of paper about 5-6 in (12.5-15 cm) wide and 6-8 in (15-20 cm) long. Fold in half lengthwise, making a soft fold.

2 Using sharp scissors, cut into the fold keeping the cuts close together, to within about ¾ in (2 cm) of the edge of the paper.

3 Wind the paper frill around your finger, allowing enough space for the cutlet bone or drumstick bone, attaching the ends with a dab of glue or sticky tape. For a ham bone, make the frill in the same way, but much deeper and longer.

For a really attractive presentation, place these cheese balls in a straw basket and garnish with fresh vine leaves and grapes. Either serve them as an appetizer or as a decorative part of a cheese course.

Herbed Soft Cheese Balls

Ingredients

MAKES 20-25

1 cup (8 oz/225 g) low-fat soft cheese or
  natural Quark
1 cup (4 oz/100 g) Cheshire or Cheddar
  cheese, finely grated
2 tablespoons dry white wine
3 tablespoons finely chopped mixed fresh
  chives, parsley, thyme and basil
salt and freshly ground white pepper

Soft Blue Cheese Balls

Ingredients

MAKES 20-25

1½ cups (12 oz/350 g) cottage cheese
1 cup (4 oz/100 g) blue cheese, crumbled
6 tablespoons (3 fl oz/100 ml) double (heavy)
  cream, whipped

salt and freshly ground white pepper
4 tablespoons finely chopped mixed fresh
  parsley, chervil and chives

1 Combine all the ingredients very thoroughly in a medium bowl. Cover and chill the mixture for 2 hours until firm. Shape the cheese mixture into small balls, rolling them between wetted hands. Cover and chill.

1 Blend together the cottage cheese and blue cheese in a medium bowl. Add the cream, then season with the salt, pepper and 1 tablespoon of the mixed herbs. Stir well to mix. Cover and chill for 2 hours until firm.

2 Shape the cheese into small balls between wetted hands and roll each one in the remaining herbs to coat completely. Cover and chill.

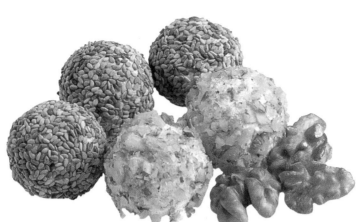

Walnut Cheese Balls

Ingredients

MAKES 20-25
1½ cups (12 oz/350 g) cream cheese, softened
½ cup (2 oz/50 g) Cheddar cheese, finely
  grated
½ cup (2 oz/50 g) fresh Parmesan cheese,
  finely grated
1 teaspoon Dijon mustard
pinch of cayenne pepper
salt and freshly ground white pepper
½ cup (2 oz/50 g) walnuts, finely chopped

Cream Cheese and Sesame Seed Balls

Ingredients

MAKES 20-25
1 cup (8 oz/225 g) cream cheese, softened
1 cup (4 oz/100 g) mature Cheddar cheese,
  grated
1 tablespoon finely chopped red pepper
1 tablespoon finely chopped green pepper

1 tablespoon finely chopped onion
1 teaspoon Worcestershire sauce
pinch of cayenne pepper
salt, to taste
toasted sesame seeds, to garnish

1 Combine all the ingredients, except the walnuts, in a medium bowl. Cover and chill the mixture for 2 hours until firm. Shape the cheese into small balls between wetted hands and roll each one in the chopped walnuts to coat completely. Cover and chill.

1 Blend the cheeses in a medium bowl. Mix in the remaining ingredients, except the sesame seeds. Cover and chill the mixture for 2 hours until firm.

2 Shape the cheese into small balls between wetted hands and roll each one in the sesame seeds to coat completely. Cover and chill.

Use the mimosa to brighten up salad leaves by sprinkling on separate layers of egg yolk and white. It is especially good on a crab salad, and dressed crab. This is also the traditional accompaniment to caviar – the sieved egg yolk and white are served in separate bowls. Use the polonaise as a topping for hot vegetables, such as cauliflower, broccoli, asparagus, etc.

1 For each *mimosa* garnish, hard-cook (hard-boil) 1 egg, then immediately cool under cold running water. Shell, then separate the egg yolk from the white. Place the egg yolk in a fine sieve. Using either the base of a ladle or your hand, push the yolk through the sieve on to a chopping board. Keep the sieve raised so the sieved yolks do not get compressed.

2 Set the yolk aside, then clean and dry the sieve. Repeat for the egg white, keeping it separate from the yolk. When completed, fluff up both the yolk and white with a fork before using.

3 For a *polonaise* garnish, fry 4 tablespoons dry white breadcrumbs in ¼ cup (2 oz/50 g) butter until golden brown. Add 1 teaspoon lemon juice, 2 tablespoons finely chopped parsley, and salt and pepper, and mix with 2 finely chopped hard-boiled eggs.

Devilled Stuffed Eggs

The following basic recipe can be varied in many ways. Instead of mayonnaise, the moistening ingredient can be softened butter, curd cheese, Greek yogurt, soured cream or crème fraîche. Vary seasonings by using fresh herbs, chopped capers or anchovies, Worcestershire sauce, soy sauce or Tabasco hot pepper sauce. As a garnish, use fresh herb sprigs, small spoonfuls of fish roe, a sprinkling of paprika or finely chopped nuts. Stuffed eggs are perfect for garnishing cold salad platters as a main course.

Ingredients

MAKES 12
6 hard-boiled (hard-cooked) eggs
3-4 tablespoons good-quality mayonnaise
1 teaspoon Dijon mustard
¼ teaspoon paprika
pinch of curry powder
salt and freshly ground white pepper
small diamonds of pimento or chopped
   blanched pistachios

1 Cut the eggs in half lengthwise. Cut a small slice from the base of each egg half, so that it will stand steady.

2 Remove the yolks and press through a sieve into a medium bowl. Blend in the mayonnaise, mustard, paprika, curry powder, salt and pepper.

3 Place the yolk mixture in a piping (pastry) bag fitted with a star nozzle (tube) and pipe an equal amount into each egg white half. Garnish with the pimento or pistachios.

Marbled Tea Eggs

*T*hese eggs are usually served as part of a selection of hors d'oeuvre or they may garnish a Chinese cold platter. The special ingredients can be bought at oriental food stores.

Ingredients

MAKES 12

1 piece of dried orange peel
12 eggs, at room temperature
¼ cup (2 oz/50 g) Chinese Keemum black
  tea leaves (strong black Chinese tea leaves)
¼ cup (2 fl oz/50 ml) dark soy sauce
2 whole star anise
2 tablespoons granulated sugar
1 tablespoon Szechuan peppercorns
1 tablespoon coarse salt

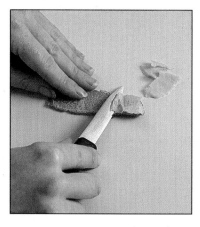

1 Soak the dried orange peel in warm water to cover until softened, about 30 minutes. Scrape the peel with a small sharp knife to remove any white pith.

2 Meanwhile, place the eggs in a large saucepan with cold water to cover and bring to simmer point over moderate heat. Reduce the heat, cover and gently simmer for 15 minutes. Remove the eggs, reserving the water. Immediately cool the eggs under cold running water for 5 minutes. Gently tap the eggs all over with the back of a spoon to crack the shells, but do not remove them.

3 Bring the reserved water to the boil. Stir in the softened orange peel and remaining ingredients. Add the eggs; if there is not enough liquid to cover them, add more water. Gently simmer the eggs, covered, for 1 hour or until the shells are a rich brown. Remove the pan from the heat and leave the eggs in the liquid for at least 1 hour, or refrigerate overnight. To serve, shell the eggs and serve whole, halved or quartered, at room temperature.

Shrimp Butterflies

Use only large, freshly cooked prawns (jumbo shrimp) – avoid frozen prawns as they can be watery and rather insipid. Use these prawns to garnish seafood cocktails, platters, salads and fish pâtés, or simply dip into a thick savoury sauce.

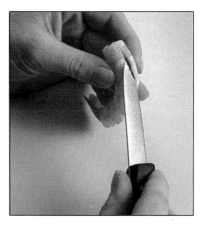

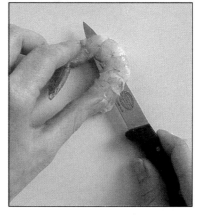

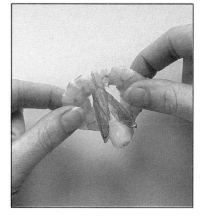

1 Peel the prawn (shrimp), leaving the tail intact. Using a small sharp knife, make a cut along the back of the prawn and remove the black vein, taking care not to damage the flesh.

2 Lay the prawn on its side and, using the small knife, slice through the back of the prawn. Do not slice the tail and the meat at the head.

3 Turn the prawn over, so the back is facing up, and gently open out to form the butterfly shape. Gently press the flesh to flatten it slightly. The tail will curl into position.

Shrimp Crowns

These are ideal to garnish warm seafood salads or served as part of a seafood appetizer. If not using the crowns as an appetizer, fill the centre with a complementary food or simply with watercress. Use large uncooked prawns (jumbo shrimp) with heads removed.

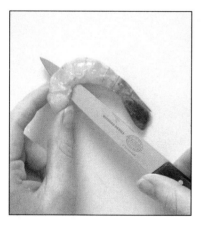

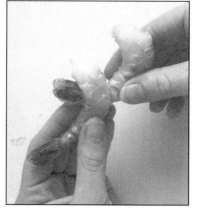

1 Peel the prawns (shrimp), leaving the tails intact. Lay a prawn on one side and make a ½ in (1 cm) lengthwise cut through the body near the head. Repeat for all the prawns.

2 Insert the tail of one prawn through one cut prawn so that the tail protrudes through the cut. Repeat with 3 more prawns, pushing the tail through a cut prawn. When you have used 5 prawns, connect the first and last prawn to make a circle.

3 Poach the crown in gently simmering court bouillon, fish stock or white wine until just pink. Drain well before using.

Use these special occasion butterflies as a garnish for cooked lobster, cold seafood salads and pâtés, or lobster soufflé. Use the legs, antennae and portions from the tail shell of a cooked lobster.

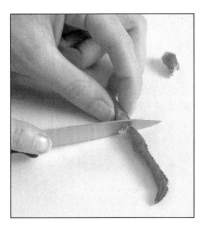

1 Take a thin leg from a cooked lobster and cut off and discard the claw. Push 2 antennae into the hollow part of it to make a long 'body'.

2 Cut off the tail piece of the lobster using a sharp, heavy knife.

3 Hold the centre of the tail piece firmly and pull off the two side pieces to form the wings of the butterfly. Push a cocktail stick (toothpick) through the centre joint of the body and position a wing on either side.

Savoury Sauce Feathering

It is important to remember that for feathering two different sauces are required, which should complement each other in terms of both flavour and colour. One light and one dark sauce give the best effect.

1 For a 3-ring feathered sauce, pour the first sauce on to a heated individual plate, swivelling the plate so that the sauce coats the base. Place the second sauce in a small greaseproof paper piping (waxed pastry) bag. Snip off the end and pipe 3 concentric circles on to the first sauce.

2 Using a skewer, draw it across the sauce from the outside edge to the centre at regular intervals to give an attractive effect. Wipe the skewer clean after each line drawn.

3 Alternatively, place small teaspoons of sauce at regular intervals around the edge of the bowl. Draw a fine skewer through the sauce to form a leaf effect.

Savoury Sauce Garnishes

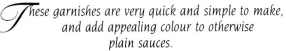

These garnishes are very quick and simple to make, and add appealing colour to otherwise plain sauces.

1 A garnish of finely diced cooked vegetables strewn over a sauce makes all the difference to the finished dish. Keep the dice fine and even. For example, a dice of courgettes (zucchini) and carrots or red pepper and chives complements and lifts a cream coloured sauce for white fish. Mounds of cooked 'baton' vegetables (thin sticks) or 'julienne' vegetables (matchsticks) are appetizing to look at and to eat.

2 Finely chopped fresh herbs, such as parsley, chives or chervil are a quick and easy way of adding colour to sauces. Either sprinkle the herbs over the sauce, or use them to make a border for it. Sprigs of herbs, especially chives, can frame a dish nicely. Use watercress for grilled (broiled) or roasted meats.

3 Fish dishes benefit from a salmon or lumpfish roe garnish or, if you can afford it, caviar. Either place small mounds artistically on the sauce or, in the case of salmon roe, carefully place each fish egg in a curved line following the plate, to give a beadlike effect.

The royale garnish is a classic addition to clear soups. It is a cooked savoury custard which is made into decorative shapes, such as tiny dice, small diamonds, squares or stars, using small cutters. The golden colour of the royale can be varied by adding a small amount of spinach, pea or asparagus purée for a green colour, puréed cooked carrots for orange, or a tomato purée to the egg mixture before cooking. The Brunoise garnish is traditional with consommé, which looks most attractive and makes a truly elegant starter when served in special consommé cups.

Royale

Ingredients

4 eggs, beaten
1 cup (8 fl oz/250 ml) milk
1 cup (8 fl oz/250 ml) hot, clear, fat free beef, chicken or fish stock, depending on soup
salt
pinch of freshly grated nutmeg (optional)

1 Preheat the oven to 325F (170C/Gas 3). Strain the eggs through a very fine strainer into a medium bowl. Gently stir in the remaining ingredients with a whisk, trying to avoid bubbles forming in the mixture.

2 Line a shallow cake tin (pan) with buttered greaseproof (waxed) paper. Carefully strain the mixture through a sieve into the tin, then place in a bain-marie filled with hot water. Bake in the oven for 30 minutes or until the mixture is set.

3 Allow to cool, then unmould carefully by lifting out the custard with the paper lining. Cut into fancy shapes with small decorative cutters. Scatter a few of the shapes over each portion of clear soup.

Brunoise

Ingredients

SERVES 4
2 oz (50 g) young carrot, peeled
2 oz (50 g) young white turnip, peeled
1 leek, white part only
1 celery stick (stalk)
2 tablespoons beef or chicken stock
12 small fresh chervil leaves

1 Cut the carrot, turnip, leek and celery into tiny, even-sized dice.

2 Place the vegetables in a small frying pan (skillet) with the stock. Cook, stirring frequently, over a low heat until the vegetables are just tender.

3 Remove from the heat and stir in the chervil leaves. Garnish each portion of soup with 2 teaspoons of the brunoise.

3

Bread and Pastry Garnishes

All kinds of bread — chunks of crusty French loaf, flat pittas with their useful pockets, crisp melba toast — are popular accompaniments to food worldwide. But garnishes made with bread have an appeal all their own: crunchy little croûtons to sprinkle over soup, or crisp larger croûtes for a casserole topping or canapé base. A simply made pancake batter is one of the easiest and most versatile basic mixtures for all kinds of mouth-watering crêpes. Filo sheets make the lightest of pastries, enclosing savoury and sweet fillings which can be varied endlessly to taste.

*S*alads and cream soups almost beg for the crunchiness of croûtons. They also make an excellent garnish for scrambled eggs, omelettes and casseroles. Croûtons keep crisp stored in an airtight tin.

1 For *plain croûtons*, cut day-old or stale slices of white or wholewheat bread into small, even cubes or small shapes. Fry the cubes in a mixture of hot butter and oil in a frying pan (skillet), stirring frequently, until evenly browned. Drain the croûtons on kitchen paper towels.

2 For *herb-flavoured croûtons*, fry as for plain croûtons and, while hot, drop into a paper bag containing salt, paprika and finely chopped (minced) fresh herbs. Close the bag and shake it until the croûtons are evenly coated. For *cheese croûtons*, substitute grated fresh Parmesan cheese for the herbs.

3 For *garlic croûtons*, cook as for plain croûtons but add finely crushed (minced) garlic to the hot butter and oil mixture.

Use to garnish party casseroles like Coq au vin, Boeuf Bourguignon or Osso Buco, and as a base for grilled tournedos or tiny roast game birds, such as quail.

1 Cut slices of bread into halves diagonally. Remove the crusts and trim each half to obtain a more pointed triangle. Trim each piece into the shape of a heart. Fry the croûtes in a mixture of hot butter and oil in a frying pan (skillet) until golden brown.

2 Dip the tip of each croûte in the sauce of the dish it is to be served with and then into a small bowl of finely chopped fresh parsley. The parsley adheres to the bread and forms a decorative point. Arrange the croûtes attractively, parsley tips uppermost, around the edge of the casserole dish.

3 For various shaped *canapé bases* cut from bread, use decorative cutters. Round, square or diamond-shaped bases are the most common and easily handled. Fry the bases in a mixture of hot butter and oil in a frying pan (skillet) until golden brown. Alternatively, grill (broil) until golden brown. Allow to cool before covering with the canapé topping.

These delicious crisp pancake rolls make a delightful edible garnish to a Chinese banquet. They are also good to serve with drinks, or as part of a selection of starters for a Chinese meal. A mixture of minced pork, sliced button mushrooms, water chestnuts and bean sprouts stir-fried with soy sauce would make an excellent filling.

Ingredients

MAKES *about* 12

1¼ *cups (5 oz/150 g) plain (all-purpose) flour*
2 *eggs, at room temperature, lightly beaten*
½ *cup (4 fl oz/120 ml) milk, at room*
   temperature
½ *cup (4 fl oz/120 ml) water*
salt
½ *cup (4 fl oz/120 ml) clarified butter*

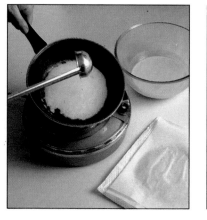

1 Sift the flour into a mixing bowl and make a well in the centre. Add the eggs and gradually stir in the flour, milk and water, to make a smooth batter. Cover the bowl and leave to stand at room temperature for 1 hour. Heat 1 tablespoon of the butter in a 6 in (15 cm) non-stick frying pan (skillet) over a medium-low heat. Ladle 3 tablespoons of the batter into the pan, tilting the pan until the base is covered with a thin layer. Cook for 1 minute.

2 Turn out the crêpe on to a kitchen paper towel and cover with greaseproof (waxed) paper. Repeat with the remaining batter, adding 1-2 tablespoons of butter to the pan as necessary. Arrange 2 tablespoons of cooked crêpe filling in the centre of the cooked side of each crêpe. Fold the bottom edge over the filling. Fold the sides over slightly, then roll up to enclose the filling.

3 Heat the remaining butter in a large frying pan over a moderate heat. Add the filled crêpes, in batches if necessary, seam side down. Cook on both sides for about 4 minutes until brown and crisp. To serve, tie half the crêpes around the centre with thin ribbons of blanched spring onion (scallion). Tie the remaining crêpes around the centre with thin ribbons of blanched carrot.

Sack Bundles

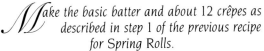

Make the basic batter and about 12 crêpes as described in step 1 of the previous recipe for Spring Rolls.

1 Make the crêpes and the cooked crêpe filling of your choice. Arrange 1½ tablespoons of the filling in the centre of the uncooked side of each crêpe.

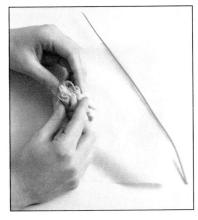

2 Gather each crêpe up like a sack and tie each bundle loosely with a chive spear. (A second pair of hands to help do this tie is helpful.)

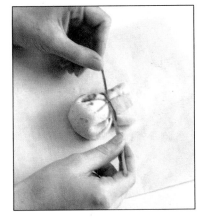

3 Place the crêpes in a greased shallow baking dish. Cook in a preheated 350F (180C/Gas 4) oven for about 5 minutes until just heated through.

Wafer-thin filo pastry, widely used in savoury and sweet dishes in Greek and Middle Eastern cooking, is now readily available in packets. Filo pastry freezes very well. Remember to keep the filo sheets you are not immediately working with covered with clingfilm (plastic wrap) or a damp cloth to prevent them from drying out, which can happen very quickly, making the pastry brittle and impossible to use. Filo pastry adapts well to a variety of shapes: apart from those given here, triangles and cigars are very popular.

Ingredients

MAKES 4
4 large sheets filo pastry
¼ cup (2 oz/50 g) butter, melted

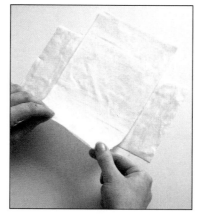

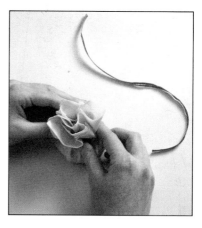

1 Preheat the oven to 400F (200C/Gas 6). Cut 1 sheet of filo pastry in half. Using a wide, soft brush and working quickly, brush 1 side of each half with some of the melted butter. Place 1 half-sheet on top of the other and, using scissors, cut them into 2 equal rectangles of 2 layers.

2 With the buttered side down, lay 1 double rectangle over the other to make a cross. At this point, mound the filling in the centre of the rectangle.

3 Gather up the pastry ends and pinch firmly around the filling to give a sack shape. Leave the pointed ends free. Repeat this process for the remaining sacks. Bake on the top shelf of the oven for 10-12 minutes until the frills are well browned. Remove from oven and tie each sack with a satin ribbon. These would be delicious filled with a mixture of curd cheese, crumbled feta cheese, chopped cooked spinach and parsley or mint.

A perfect garnish to set off a Middle Eastern style dish, Filo Baskets can be filled with a creamy cheese mixture and topped with chopped fresh chives or thinly shredded leeks.

1 Preheat the oven to 375F (190C/Gas 5). For one basket, take one large sheet of filo pastry and brush all over with melted butter.

2 Cut the sheet into 4 pieces and pile one on top of another, arranging each piece at a different angle. Brush a little more melted butter over the top piece of pastry. Press the pastry layers into a buttered 6 in (15 cm) ovenproof gratin dish.

3 Transfer the filled dish to a baking sheet and support the edges of the pastry with pieces of foil. Bake in the oven for 15-20 minutes until the pastry is golden. Spoon in the chosen sweet or savoury filling. If liked, trim the pastry edges with pinking shears for a decorative touch. Chopped mango or crystallized ginger mixed with Greek yogurt would be delicious for a sweet filling: serve immediately.

Before you bake your pie, tart or flan (either sweet or savoury), decorate it with scraps of leftover pastry. After decorating, refrigerate for 10 minutes as the chilling will help keep the shape.

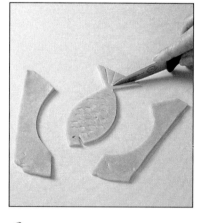

1 Use small pastry cutters to stamp out shapes, cut out shapes with a knife or mould them freehand. Choose shapes which reflect the filling – a bouquet of little vegetables for a vegetable pie, fish shapes for fish pies, holly leaf shapes for a turkey pie at Christmas, etc. For *leaves*, use a leaf-shaped cutter or cut the pastry into strips, then cut diagonally into even-sized diamonds. Mark the veins of the leaf with the blade of a knife.

2 *Apple pies* can be decorated with a leafy apple branch, with small balls of pastry made to look like apples. For *puff pastry fleurons (crescents)*, which are the classic French garnish for fish or seafood dishes, roll out puff pastry ⅛ in (3 mm) thick. Brush the dough with beaten egg. Cut into fleurons using a small fluted crescent-shaped cutter. Leave the fleurons to rest for 20 minutes. Bake in a preheated 425F (220C/Gas 7) oven for 10 minutes.

3 For a *fish-shaped* pie decoration, use a small sharp knife to score out the tail markings and mouth in shortcrust pastry. Use the point of the knife to score semi-circles into the pastry to imitate the fish scales.

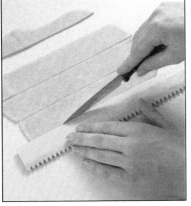

4 To make *chrysanthemums*, cut strips of shortcrust pastry (basic pie dough) 6 × 2 in (15 × 5 cm), using a ruler to keep the cutting edge straight.

5 Start cutting short slits along one side, gradually making them longer. Brush with beaten egg.

6 Roll up the pastry, starting from the long cuts end. Ease the fronds apart, then sit the chrysanthemums upright on the pie vent.

4

Fruit Garnishes

The joy of garnishing with fresh fruit is that it lends itself so naturally to both sweet and savoury dishes. In the following pages you will find some exquisite and decorative ideas for fruit garnishes, including Apricot Roses, Apple Wings, Strawberry Fans and Fig Flowers. There are even some special suggestions on how to make the most of citrus fruit, as it is readily available and stores well. But whatever your need, you can be sure of finding a fruit — and garnish — for every season.

Apple Wings

Use to decorate fruit and cheese platters. An assortment of different coloured apples – red, green and yellow – looks particularly attractive.

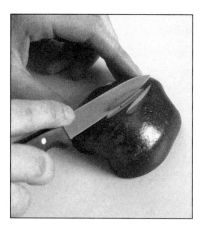

1 Halve an apple lengthwise and place cut side down on a chopping board. Make a small diagonal cut into the centre of the apple; then make another cut in the opposite direction and lift out the wedge.

2 Continue to cut the apple, following the lines of the first cut, and remove each piece as it is cut until there are 2 wedges of the apple left.

3 Reshape the apple half back into the original form. Gently move each apple slice to separate and then open the bottom wedges to form wings.

Apple Swans

A sure way of encouraging children to eat more fruit is to produce these unusual swans. They're great fun to make, too.

1 Cut a ½ in (1 cm) slice off one side of a large eating apple. Place the slice cut side down on a chopping board and, using a small sharp knife, mark out a head and neck in one complete piece the full length of the apple slice. The head can be looking up or down, but keep the beak part pointed. Carve it out, sprinkle with lemon juice and set aside.

2 To attach neck and head to body, using the point of the knife, make a hole at the front of the apple to hold the neck in place. Insert the neck and adjust until it fits snugly. Remove the neck and set aside. On one side of the apple, cut thin wedges by first holding the knife vertically and slicing down and then holding the knife horizontally and slicing across. Remove 5 wedges for each wing. Repeat on the other side of the apple to make the other wing.

3 Put the wedges back together and push them towards the back of the swan so they are staggered and simulate the wings. Place the head on the swan and sprinkle the whole apple with lemon juice to prevent discoloration.

These look effective on a glossy chocolate cake or chiffon pie, or as decoration for a creamy fruit mousse or fool. The apricot roses could also be served as a sweetmeat with after-dinner coffee.

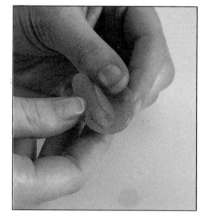

1 Use 3 or 4 moist dried apricots for each rose. Carefully slice each apricot in half, using a small sharp knife.

2 Using a rolling pin, roll each apricot half out between 2 sheets of greaseproof (waxed) paper to a thickness of 1/16 in (1 mm). Roll one up tightly, sticky side in, to form the centre bud of a rose.

3 Wrap another apricot half around the bud, sticky side in, pressing gently to adhere. Repeat with 2 more apricots, overlapping half the previous one. Gently bend the top of the outer 3 apricots outwards to form petals. Place a cocktail stick (toothpick) horizontally through the base of the rose, to hold the petals in place. Cut off the apricot below the cocktail stick to form a flat base. Freeze the roses on a plate for 30 minutes. Discard the cocktail sticks.

Grapefruit Wedges

Use either yellow or rosy-pink grapefruit for these wedges or a mixture of the two — they are perfect for fruit salads or breakfast fruit cups. Try adding the grapefruit wedges to cottage cheese with other sliced fruit such as peaches and strawberries: served on a bed of crisp shredded lettuce and topped with a sprinkling of nuts this makes a healthy, delicious lunch. Oranges can be prepared and used in the same way as grapefruit.

1 Using a sharp knife, peel the skin and all the white pith from the fruit.

2 Make a cut into the fruit, slicing very close to the membrane of one of the segments. Make another cut, slicing next to the membrane on the other side of the segment. Lift out the segment. Repeat all the way around the fruit.

3 Once all the fruit has been removed, squeeze any juice from the remaining membranes over the fruit.

Lemon Pigs

These are fun for parties: spear the pig with a selection of titbits on cocktail sticks (toothpicks), such as cubes of cheese with pineapple chunks or baby cocktail onions, parma ham rolled round balls of melon, etc.

1 Choose a lemon with a nice pointed 'nose'. Use a cocktail stick (toothpick) to make a hole on each side of the nose and fill each with a black peppercorn, clove, or piece of black olive.

2 Cut a little wedge in the centre of the nose to imitate the mouth. Cut an 'ear' on each side of the lemon. The tail can be made from a piece of curly parsley.

3 Place 4 cocktail sticks (toothpicks) underneath the lemon pig for the legs.

Use citrus baskets to garnish fish or chicken platters. The centres can be filled with salad greens or the segments of the fruit. Small melons can be treated in the same fashion, with the seeds removed.

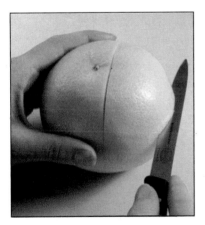

1 Use a blemish-free citrus fruit. Place the fruit on its side and cut halfway down, slightly off centre. Make a horizontal cut towards the base of the first cut.

2 Repeat the process on the other side; lift out the wedges of fruit. For a different effect, make zigzag cuts, rather than straight ones.

3 Cut away the flesh under the handle and scoop it out of the base.

A canelle (grooving) knife can also be used for decorative edges for vegetables such as cucumbers and mushrooms.

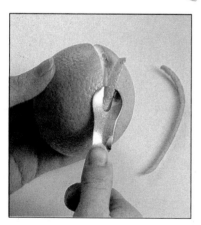

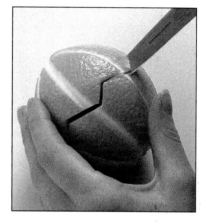

1 Make evenly spaced vertical grooved cuts around the fruit with a canelle (grooving) knife.

2 Cut the fruit in half crosswise. For an extra-decorative effect, cut in half zigzag style, making short, deep diagonal cuts in either direction all the way round the middle of the fruit, then gently twist the two halves apart.

3 Or the fruit can be sliced – ¼ in (5mm) thick if the slices are to lay flat or ⅛ in (3 mm) thick for twists. The flat slices can be cut into halves, quarters or eighths. They look good as a garnish for a pâté, together with a bay leaf.

Mango Hedgehog

A dish of curry, especially chicken or lamb, would benefit from this attractive mango garnish. Place the hedgehog in the centre of the serving platter, and spoon the curry around it.

1 Slice off the 2 fleshy sides from a mango, cutting close to the large stone (pit). Place one side, skin-side down, on a chopping board. Cut the flesh into evenly spaced diagonal lines, taking care not to cut through the skin.

2 Cut the flesh of the same mango side in the opposite direction, making more evenly spaced diagonal lines so the cuts form a diamond pattern. Repeat the diagonal cuts with the other mango side.

3 Hold one cut mango in both hands and push upward so the shape is reversed and the cuts are spread out. Repeat for the other mango side.

In the Caribbean a selection of beautifully cut fruits is often served for breakfast, arranged on a platter over crushed ice. These fresh, colourful fruits would look equally good garnishing all manner of creamy desserts.

1 Starfruit (carambola) is simply thinly sliced, then used to decorate ice cream, iced (frosted) cakes, tarts and flans or folded into fruit salads.

2 Cut the ends off a kiwifruit (Chinese gooseberry). Peel away the fuzzy skin with a small sharp knife or vegetable peeler and discard. Thinly slice the fruit. Decorate cream flans, mousses or fruit salads with the sliced kiwifruit, or add to a green salad for extra interest.

3 Cut a zigzag through to the centre of a passionfruit, or simply slice straight through. Twist the halves apart. The decorative yellow/green seeds inside are edible.

Ripe, luscious purple figs with their crimson centres make a perfect centrepiece for a summer dessert. Prepared in the same way, fig flowers go beautifully with parma ham for a starter, as a change from the more usual accompanying melon.

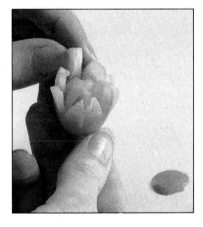

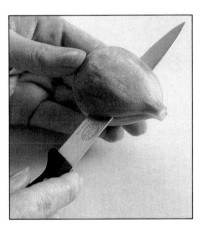

1 Make a cut from the pointed end halfway through the fig.

2 Turn the fig 90° and make another cut from the pointed end halfway through the fig. Push the 4 wedges open from the centre. For more 'petals', make a total of 4 cuts, instead of 2. Top with Greek yogurt or whipped cream and a fruit flavoured coulis or fruit purée.

3 Kumquats can be prepared in the same way, but cut a small piece from the stalk (stem) end to level it before making the 2 cuts.

Frosted Grapes

Cakes, cold soufflés and other sweet desserts could benefit from this effective decoration. Frosted grapes also look pretty in small sweet cases, served with petits fours as an accompaniment to after-dinner coffee. Be sure to choose large seedless grapes. Clusters of red- and blackcurrants can be frosted in the same way.

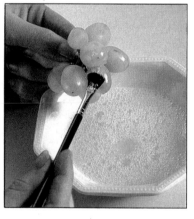

1 Wash grapes, green or purple, and dry thoroughly. Snip into small clusters with scissors.

2 Beat an egg white and 1 tablespoon lemon juice with a fork just until small bubbles form. Use a fine brush to paint the mixture on to the grapes. Make sure the grapes are thoroughly coated.

3 Place the cluster of grapes on a sheet of greaseproof (waxed) paper, dusted thickly with caster (superfine) sugar. Using a fine sieve, thickly dust more sugar over the grapes. Shake off the excess sugar and place the grapes on a wire rack to dry.

Use this attractive basket as a container for fruit salads, ice cream or even a summer punch. Chill well in the refrigerator before serving. Any leftover melon removed from the inside can be whizzed in a blender with fresh fruit juice and served in tumblers over cracked ice as a refreshing long drink.

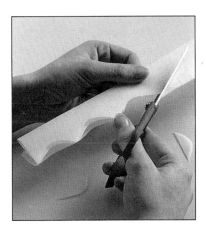

1 Level the bottom of the watermelon with a sharp knife. Fold a long strip of greaseproof (waxed) paper in half, then fold in half again. Cut along the length with scissors to make a pattern for the handle of the basket. Unfold the strip, place on top of the watermelon and secure with cocktail sticks (toothpicks). Outline the handle with the point of a small sharp knife.

2 Use the same template to mark the top edge of the basket. Mark the outline with a small sharp knife. Remove the template and cut out the two lids. Scoop out the flesh and seeds from inside the watermelon.

3 Cut another paper template for the design to be carved on the side of the melon. Anchor the template with cocktail sticks (toothpicks) and score the outline with a small sharp knife. Carve out the peel to reveal the white pith. Fill the basket with fruit. Use the lids to cover the basket until served.

Melon Balls and Leaves

Use in melon baskets, starter cocktails, fruit salads or as a garnish for raw hams, such as prosciutto or parma. The leaves look pretty as a side garnish to platters of meat or fruit. These are good ways of using up a portion of leftover melon.

1 Cut a melon in half widthwise, then remove the seeds with a teaspoon.

2 For *melon balls*, using a melon baller, cup side facing the fruit, push the melon baller into the flesh. Twist right around so that the cup faces upward, then remove the melon baller from the flesh. Push out the ball of fruit, then continue making more melon balls.

3 For *melon leaves*, use a thin flat slice each from a honeydew melon and a canteloupe melon. Cut equal half leaf shapes from both slices. Place the flat side of a green shape against the flat side of an orange shape to form a melon leaf.

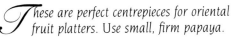

These are perfect centrepieces for oriental fruit platters. Use small, firm papaya.

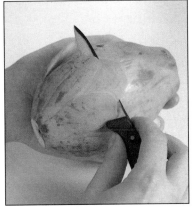

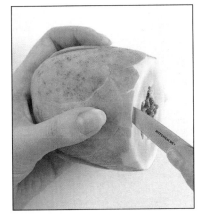

1 Level the base of the papaya so that it stands upright. Using a small sharp knife, make downward slits from the middle of the fruit almost to the base, to create the bottom 5 petals.

2 Cut a second row of petals in the same way, just above the bottom row. Slice off the top of the papaya ½ in (1 cm) above the top row of petals.

3 Cut a final row of small petals to reach the rim. Remove excess peel between the top petals. Carefully scoop out the pips from the centre and reserve. Remove and discard the flesh, creating a hollowed-out shell. Replace the pips in the centre and gently bend back the petals to create a flower.

The pineapple needs to be very ripe for this garnish, which looks good on a buffet table.

1 Trim two-thirds from the leafy green top of a chilled, ripe pineapple. Cut the fruit into 8 lengthwise wedges.

2 Cut off the core and discard. Using a sharp knife, pare the skin in one piece, leaving it in place.

3 Cut the pulp downwards into 5-6 slices, retaining a boat shape. Stagger the slices for a more attractive finish.

Strawberry Fans

Use for decorating desserts, ice cream and sundaes, or serve with smoked chicken or turkey. A savoury summer side salad of sliced strawberries, sliced cucumber and chopped fresh mint, garnished with strawberry fans, would be delightful.

1 Choose firm red strawberries. Place a strawberry on its side on a chopping board and make 5-7 cuts in the fruit, taking care not to slice right through to the top of the berry.

2 Using the flat side of a large knife, gently press on the strawberry to 'fan' it out.

3 With the point of a knife, carefully cut or pull out the centre hull. Replace it with a small sprig of fresh mint.

5

Sweet Garnishes

This section contains lots of ideas for party cooks. Some of the recipes, for example Caramelized Fruits and Chocolate Cups, are perfect for serving with after-dinner coffee and could replace a dessert course at the end of a dinner party. Others, like Brandy Snap Baskets and Caramel Cages, give a new look to the presentation of tried and tested dessert favourites like ice cream, sorbet or chocolate mousse. Everyone who enjoys making desserts, cakes and sweets enjoys decorating them too, and will find plenty to inspire them here. Chocolate is a particularly versatile decorative ingredient, and the most is made of it in this chapter, with chocolate leaves and curls, and solid and outline shapes.

Use these crisp cases to hold ice cream, sorbet, fruit and/or whipped cream or cream fillings. Fill the baskets just before serving.

Ingredients

MAKES 10

3 tablespoons (2 oz/50 g) golden (corn) syrup
¼ cup (2 oz/50 g) caster (superfine) sugar
¼ cup (2 oz/50 g) butter
½ cup (2 oz/50 g) plain (all-purpose) flour
1 teaspoon ground ginger
finely grated zest of 1 lemon

1 Preheat the oven to 350F (180C/ Gas 4). Cut out ten 6 in (15 cm) squares of greaseproof (waxed) paper. Place the paper on baking sheets. Warm the syrup, sugar and butter in a saucepan over gentle heat. Sift the flour and ginger together and stir into the pan with the lemon zest. Remove immediately from the heat.

2 Drop a tablespoon of the mixture onto the centre of each paper square, spreading the mixture with a palette knife (or metal spatula) if necessary. Bake in the oven for 7 minutes or until the biscuits (cookies) are a dark golden brown.

3 Remove the biscuits from the oven and leave to stand for 1 minute. Place the biscuits over the bases of lightly greased glasses and press the biscuit down so it takes the shape of the glass to form a cup. Gently peel off the paper. Allow to cool before storing in an airtight container.

Hazelnut Cones

Filled with scoops of ice cream, whipped cream or low-fat soft cheese, these cones make sensational garnishes for fruit desserts. Top with grated chocolate or fresh berry fruits.

Ingredients

MAKES 30-32

4 size 1-2 (large) egg whites

¾ cup plus 2 tablespoons (7 oz/200 g) caster (superfine) sugar

1 cup (4 oz/100 g) plain (all-purpose) flour, sifted with ½ teaspoon salt

½ cup (4 oz/100 g) butter, melted and cooled

½ cup (2 oz/50 g) ground, lightly toasted hazelnuts

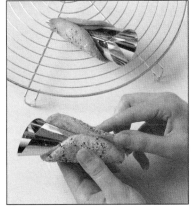

1 Preheat the oven to 375F (190C/ Gas 5). Line 3-4 large baking sheets with greaseproof (waxed) paper. Whisk the egg whites in a bowl until frothy, then add the sugar and continue whisking until thick and glossy. Fold in the flour alternately with the butter until well blended.

2 Put dessertspoons of the mixture on the baking sheets, 3-4 at a time, and spread into thin rounds, each about 4 in (10 cm) across. Sprinkle each with a small amount of ground toasted hazelnuts.

3 Bake in the oven for 8-9 minutes until golden and pale brown at the edges. Allow to cool for a few seconds, then lift with a palette knife (or metal spatula) and fold quickly around a metal cone mould. Repeat for the second biscuit (cookie) . If the second or third biscuit becomes too cool and brittle to mould, return to the oven for a few seconds to soften. Allow to cool on a wire rack. When cold, store the biscuits in an airtight container.

*U*se strawberries, mandarin segments, cherries or grapes. Serve within 4 hours of caramelizing. Nuts, especially almonds, brazils and hazelnuts, can be given the same treatment. Use Caramelized Fruits to decorate cheesecakes or gâteaux.

Basic Caramel

Ingredients

MAKES *about 2½ cups (1 pint/600 ml)*
2 cups (1 lb/450 g) sugar
½ cup (4 fl oz/120 ml) water
¼ teaspoon cream of tartar dissolved in 1 tablespoon water

1 To make caramel, put the sugar and water into a heavy saucepan, stir lightly. Bring to boiling. After 3 minutes, add the cream of tartar. Cook, but do not stir, for 10 minutes until a light caramel is formed. Use a pastry brush dipped in cold water to brush down any sugar crystals on the side of pan. Remove from heat. If the caramel continues to cook and darken too much, place the saucepan in lukewarm water. Remelt if it becomes too thick.

2 Lightly grease a baking sheet. If using cherries or grapes, wash and drain on kitchen paper towels. Clean strawberries with a pastry brush and leave the stalks (stems) on. Peel mandarins and separate the segments. Remove pith and membranes and dry the segments on a wire rack for 3-4 hours. Push a cocktail stick (toothpick) into the segments.

3 Place the saucepan of caramel in a bowl of warm water to prevent it setting. Dip the fruit in the hot caramel, allowing the excess caramel to drip back into the saucepan. Place on the baking sheet and leave until set. Serve in small petit fours cases.

Caramel Cages

These decorative cages can be used to make very special presentations of ice cream, a mousse or a fruit fool. Place the cage over the top of the dessert, or for a change, fill the cage as shown here.

1 Make the basic caramel recipe opposite. Allow the caramel to cool until thick enough to form long threads. Cover the outside of a ladle with foil and grease the foil.

2 Using a teaspoon filled with caramel, drape long threads over the top and side of the ladle. The threads should be long enough to weave back and forth from one side to the other. If the threads are too short, the cage will break when unmoulded.

3 Remove the cage from the ladle and allow to cool. Gently remove the foil from the cage.

Chocolate Boxes

hese can be decorated with Strawberry Fans (see page 101) or a small cluster of red- or blackcurrants. Assemble the boxes just before serving, so that the chocolate remains crisp.

1 Cut either a plain Madeira (butter) cake or a sponge (layer) cake into squares the same size as a square of chocolate mint. Cut each square of cake into ½ in (1 cm) slices.

2 Warm a small amount of strawberry or apricot jam, then cool slightly. Spread the jam over the sides and top of the cake squares, leaving the underside unglazed.

3 Whip cream until thickened. Just before serving, spread over each jam-glazed square of cake, covering the top and sides. Place 4 chocolate mints around each cake and pipe whipped cream on top. Decorate with fruit.

Chocolate-dipped Fruits and Nuts

Use either bittersweet, preferably imported, or plain (semisweet) chocolate melted over hot, not boiling, water. Always melt chocolate by this method and never over direct heat. Overheating makes chocolate lose its glossy smoothness: it becomes gritty and dull. Try dipping various fruits, such as cherries, orange segments, pineapple triangles, kiwifruit (Chinese gooseberry) or banana slices to make stunning garnishes for all types of dessert.

1 For *chocolate-dipped strawberries*, dip the strawberries into the melted chocolate so the coating is halfway up the side of the berry. Allow the excess chocolate to drip off, then leave to set on foil-lined trays.

2 For *chocolate-dipped dried apricots*, dip each apricot into the melted chocolate, coating the lower half. Allow the excess chocolate to drip off, then leave to set on foil-lined trays.

3 For *chocolate-dipped nuts*, such as macadamia nuts, whole almonds, hazelnuts or walnut halves, insert a cocktail stick (toothpick) into each nut. Dip the nut into the melted chocolate, then push the cocktail stick into half an orange or grapefruit to allow the chocolate to set evenly.

Chocolate Cups

*F*ill the cups with liqueurs (Tia Maria or Grand Marnier would complement the chocolate perfectly) and serve with after-dinner coffee. The cups also make dainty, rich desserts, filled with whipped rum-flavoured cream or a mixture of avocaat, cream and chopped stem ginger. Or fill with maraschino cherries or juicy black cherries with the stones (pits) removed, and pipe a swirl of cream on top.

1 Melt plain (semisweet) chocolate in a bowl over hot, not boiling water, or use a double boiler.

2 Use a small brush to paint the chocolate on the inside of small foil cases, making sure the top edge is fairly thick. Allow chocolate to set, then apply a second coating. Leave the cups in a cool place to set. Do not refrigerate or the chocolate will develop a 'bloom'.

3 Carefully peel away the foil cups with your fingers or with a skewer to separate the chocolate from the foil.

Chocolate Leaves

Chocolate leaves make an attractive and tasty decoration for all kinds of desserts and cakes. Make sure the leaves you pick have not been sprayed with an insecticide. It is essential that they are absolutely clean and dry before they are coated with chocolate.

1 Use either bittersweet, preferably imported, or plain (semisweet) chocolate, melted over hot, not boiling, water. Choose non-poisonous leaves, such as camellia or rose. Wipe clean with kitchen paper towels.

2 Either use a small brush to brush one side of the leaves with melted chocolate or dip the underside directly into the melted chocolate.

3 When the chocolate has set, peel away the leaf. For a more realistic appearance, lay the leaves, uncoated side down, over a wooden rolling pin while they set.

Outlined Chocolate Shapes

The only real challenge to outlined chocolate shapes is keeping a steady hand while piping. Use for cakes, petits fours or cream desserts. The shapes are ideal for the message on a birthday cake.

1 Draw your designs on a sheet of white paper with a black felt-tipped pen. Place a sheet of greaseproof (waxed) or silicone-coated paper on top of the sheet of paper. Pipe a small blob of chocolate between the two sheets to prevent them slipping.

2 To make a greaseproof (waxed) paper piping (pastry) bag, cut a triangle of greaseproof paper 11 × 7 in (28 × 18 cm) and place the longest edge away from you and the right angle in line with your right arm. Place your finger down the long edge and curl the left-hand corner over to meet the right-angle corner.

3 Hold these 2 points securely and curl the third point around to meet them. If the join is not exact, the bag will be very loose. Fold the 3 points to the inside and crease.

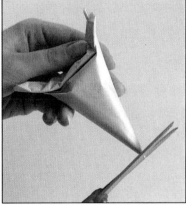

4 Make 2 small tears in the paper and fold back a lip to hold the seam. Half fill the bag with melted chocolate or icing, fold the top over and snip off.

5 Place the melted chocolate in the small greaseproof paper piping bag. Following the pattern seen through the sheet of greaseproof paper, pipe out the shapes.

6 Let the shapes harden before carefully removing from the paper with a palette knife (or metal spatula) or gently peeling the paper away.

hese look decorative on a mousse or gâteau, especially a Black Forest gâteau, a delectable combination of lightest chocolate sponge, whipped cream, kirsch and juicy black cherries.

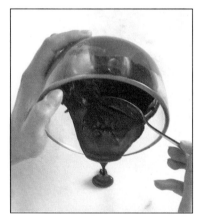

1 Melt chocolate in the top of a double boiler or in a bowl over a pan of gently simmering water. When the chocolate has melted, pour it onto a cold working surface, preferably a slab of marble.

2 Using a spatula, smooth the chocolate thinly across the marble. Leave it to stand until almost rubbery, but not hard, before curling.

3 To make curls or chocolate caraques, push a spatula (smoother) or a thin palette knife (or metal spatula) down the length of the sheet of chocolate. A thin layer of chocolate is lifted off the surface, which then curls up. You may find you need to adjust the angle of the spatula or palette knife to make thin curls.

These chocolate shapes can be used to decorate cakes and gâteaux, or iced biscuits for a children's party. Cut the chocolate when almost set.

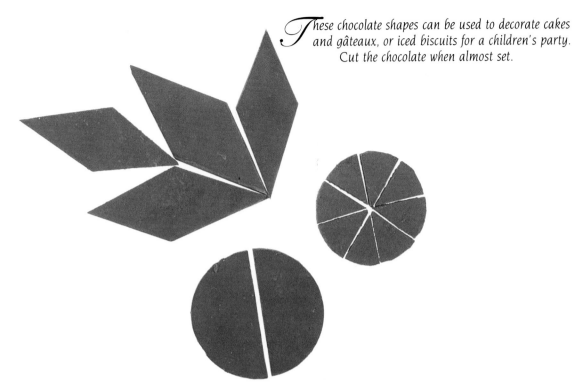

1 Pour melted chocolate onto a sheet of silicone-coated (waxed) paper. Lift the edges of the paper and tilt the chocolate in different directions until the surface is smooth and even. Leave until almost set.

2 For *squares*, use a sharp knife to cut parallel lines of your chosen width across the chocolate. Cut another set of equidistant lines at 90° to make squares. For *diamonds*, cut the second set of lines at an angle of 45°.

3 For *circles* and *rings*, cut the chocolate by pressing in a round cutter and giving a slight twist. Make rings by cutting a smaller circle inside the first.

Glazed Lemon Slices

*T*hese make a pretty, refreshing decoration for gâteaux, flans and tartlets. The tangy, sweet/sour flavour blends well with sweet ingredients and other fruits. Limes, small oranges, satsumas and tangerines can also be used.

1 Take grooves out of the fruit with a grooving (canelle) knife if liked, then cut into slices and remove any pips. Place in a large frying pan.

2 Cover with water and bring to the boil. Simmer, uncovered, for 15-20 minutes until translucent and tender. Drain the fruit very thoroughly.

3 Strain the reserved liquor into a clean pan to remove any pips. Add 3-4 oz (75-100 g) caster sugar to the liquor and stir until dissolved over a low heat. Bring to the boil and boil until reduced to a syrupy glaze. Transfer the lemon slices to a plate or tray and spoon the hot syrup over them. Leave until cold before use.

Decorative Cocktail Glasses

*A*lcoholic and non-alcoholic drinks alike look more appealing with a colourful fruit garnish, which can be enjoyed when the drink is finished.

1 Citrus twists, especially differently coloured ones, are particularly effective as a cocktail stick (toothpick) garnish. To make citrus twists, make a cut into the centre of a thin slice of lemon, lime or orange. Twist each side of the cut in opposite directions. Maraschino cherries can be inserted between the twists, if liked.

2 Many different types of fruit can be used as a garnish on a cocktail stick. Try assembling 3 different types together (for example, a small spear of papaya, a maraschino cherry and a slice of starfruit), or keeping to one type of fruit, such as different coloured melon balls (see page 98).

3 A small wedge of pineapple with the rind on, a maraschino cherry and 2-3 splayed out pineapple leaves also make an attractive cocktail stick garnish, especially for pineapple-based cocktails. When spearing the pineapple leaves, pierce the base of the leaves, rather than the tops.

*U*se to decorate cakes, desserts and chocolates with a delicate touch of natural, edible colour. A Middle Eastern-style ice cream perfumed with rosewater would look sensational served with a scattering of pink and dark red frosted rose petals. A decoration of bright marigold or chrysanthemum petals gives a pale cheesecake a special lift, and tiny frosted violets provide an ideal finishing touch for home-made chocolates.

1 Use any edible unsprayed flowers, such as violets, sweet peas, roses, freesias, chrysanthemums and marigolds. Beat an egg white with a fork until just mixed but not frothy. Use a fine brush to coat both sides of the flower petal with egg white.

2 As each flower is coated with the egg white, place on a sheet of greaseproof (waxed) paper thickly coated with caster (superfine) sugar. With a sieve, sprinkle more sugar over the top of the flower. If any parts are uncoated, carefully dab on more egg white and sprinkle wih sugar.

3 As each flower is sugared, place on a fine wire rack to dry in an airy place. If the weather is damp, place in a preheated 300F (150C/Gas 2) oven for 10 minutes. Allow to cool for 2-3 hours before using.

Flowers, fruits, herbs or even food such as unshelled prawns (shrimp), when suspended in a clear ice bowl, helps to create an attractive container for a fruit salad or iced soup or, for total luxury, a large helping of caviar.

1 Use 2 glass freezerproof bowls which, when fitted one inside the other, will leave a space of about ½ in (1 cm) between them. Fill the larger bowl one third full with cold water. Push the smaller bowl into the water and secure with sticky tape, ensuring that the 2 bowls are level. The water should now come two-thirds of the way up the bowls.

2 Push decorations into the water between the bowls. Transfer the bowls to a freezer and freeze overnight or until frozen. Add another layer of decorations, then gently pour in approximately 1 cup (8 fl oz/250 ml) cold water, or just enough to cover the decorations. Return to the freezer overnight or until frozen. Fill to the top with more ice water and freeze again.

3 To finish, unmould the bowl by filling the smaller bowl with tepid water. Twist to loosen and remove. To remove the larger bowl, dip it in tepid water, then twist to loosen. Keep the ice bowl in the freezer until ready to use.

6

Icings and Decorations

*S*pecial cakes are a popular
way of celebrating all kinds of
occasions. This chapter tells you how to decorate
a cake giving really professional-looking results. There is
advice on how to make your own icing bag and how to use
piped royal icing or moulded fondant to create a complete
range of decorative motifs — from scrolls, shells and fans
to ravishing bouquets of flowers — lilies of the valley
for a christening, orchids for a Golden Wedding
and holly and mistletoe for a Christmas cake.
There are also lots of fun decorations
for children's party cakes. Just follow
the step-by-step instructions,
have a little patience,
and your success
will be guaranteed!

Lemon and Lime Shapes

Ideal for garnishes on meat and fish dishes, shellfish and eggs, as well as for sweet dishes. Use firm citrus fruit for the best results.

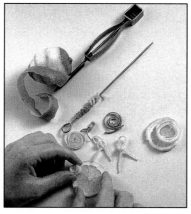

1 Pare the rind thinly from lemons and limes, using a grooving (canelle) knife, keeping the cuts equidistant all round and beginning at the top and continuing to the base. These strips of peel can be cut into narrow strips to use raw or blanched. Slice the lemons and limes to use whole, halved or twisted.

2 Pare the rind thinly from lemons and limes, using a potato peeler, and for really long twists of peel, begin at the top and work all the way to the base. Cut into narrow strips using a knife or scissors and wind tightly round skewers for corkscrew effects, tie into knots or bows and other shapes. Also slice the fruit, cut off the edge of the rind but keep it still attached to the slice and then twist this over the slice prettily.

3 Cut the thinly pared fruit rinds into shapes, using a sharp knife or aspic cutters, and use to decorate sweet and savoury dishes.

Icing Sugar Decorations

Use sifted cocoa on light coloured cakes and icing sugar on darker cakes. Select any type of leaf or pattern or doily for the design. Take extreme care when lifting the pattern off so you don't spoil the finished design.

1 Put a doily with a large pattern on a cake which has had the sides and top decorated before adding the pattern. Using a wire sieve, sift cocoa or icing sugar to give an even layer over it. With great care lift off the doily to reveal the icing sugar pattern.

2 Lay narrow strips of paper over a cake in a criss-cross design. Again sift over cocoa or icing sugar evenly. You may need help to lift off the strips of paper with great care.

3 Find pretty distinctive-shaped leaves, wash and dry thoroughly and place on the cake. Sift over cocoa or icing sugar, then remove the leaves.

Basic Marzipan

Although marzipan can be purchased ready-made, it is simple to make at home and stores well, double-wrapped, in the refrigerator. Make sure it comes to room temperature before rolling out, moulding or tinting. If you do not have time to make your own, buy white ready-made marzipan, which is much better for tinting than the yellow variety.

Ingredients

MAKES ENOUGH TO COVER A 9 *in* (23 *cm*) CAKE

2 cups (1 *lb*/450 *g*) caster (superfine) sugar
4½ cups (1 *lb*/450 *g*) icing (confectioner's) sugar
4 cups (1 *lb*/450 *g*) ground almonds
1 tablespoon rum, brandy or whisky (if the marzipan is to be kept over a long period) or few drops of lemon juice
2 size 1 (large) eggs, lightly beaten

1 Combine the sugars and almonds in a large bowl and mix thoroughly. Make a well in the centre and add the flavouring. Pour most of the egg into the well and stir with a wooden spoon to a stiff paste. You may not need all the egg – if the paste is too soft, it is difficult to handle.

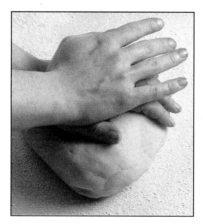

2 Work the mixture by hand and knead until well combined.

3 Turn the marzipan out onto a sugared work surface and knead until smooth. To tint marzipan, dip a cocktail stick (toothpick) in food colouring and streak the marzipan with the colouring. Knead the marzipan thoroughly until the colour is evenly distributed. If making marzipan ahead of time, store in a double wrapping of clingfilm (plastic wrap).

Marzipan Roses

Red marzipan roses would look very pretty on a white-iced St Valentine, engagement or wedding anniversary cake.

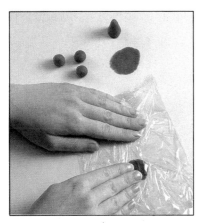

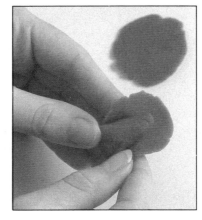

1 Roll out a ball of plain or coloured marzipan, then shape it into a cone 2 in (5 cm) long. For the petals, roll out a ball of marzipan the size of a large pea. Place the ball in a clear plastic bag or between 2 sheets of clingfilm (plastic wrap). Squash the ball with your index finger, then flatten it into a petal shape. Keep the bottom part thicker as it has to be attached to the cone. Make 5 petals for a small rose and 11-12 petals for a larger one.

2 Wrap one petal completely around the cone, keeping the top part about ¼ in (5 mm) above the cone. Squeeze the base of the petal to indent it into the cone. Place the centre edge of the second petal opposite the join line of the first petal and about ¼ in (5 mm) higher. Curl the top part of the petal back for a more natural look.

3 Keep placing petals on the rose, positioning them for a natural look and curling the top part of the petals. Then decide on the best angle for displaying the rose, then cut it off from the cone at an angle so it sits naturally.

Either use tinted marzipan for the fruit, or use white marzipan and paint it afterwards with food colouring. Little clusters of different fruits look good on a cake, or you could arrange a selection in a tiny basket and use it as a centrepiece.

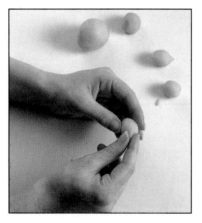

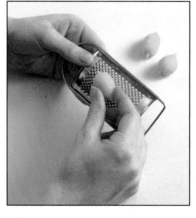

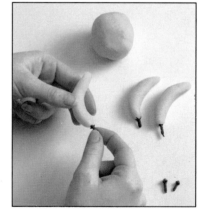

1 For a *lemon*, roll out a ball of yellow marzipan and squeeze the ends to a slight point. Indent one end to simulate the stalk (stem) end, then insert a tiny piece of green marzipan for the stalk.

2 For the appearance of *lemon peel*, finish the lemon by rolling it on a nutmeg grater. An orange can be made in the same way using orange marzipan, but keep the shape in a ball.

3 For a *banana*, roll a piece of yellow marzipan into a sausage shape. Curve the shape and flatten the sides to give it a banana shape. Paint or dust on fine brown strands of food colouring. Insert a clove for a stalk (stem).

4 For a bunch of *grapes*, roll a cone of purple or green marzipan. Make several tiny balls to represent the grapes. Arrange the grapes all over the cone to form a bunch, pressing each one in carefully.

5 You can easily make *plums, apricots* and *cherries* using appropriately coloured marzipan. Roll into a ball, then make an indent down one side to represent a crease. Using a small piece of green marzipan, make a leaf to insert in the top of the fruit.

6 Make cherries from purple or red marzipan. Roll into small balls and use a clove for the stalk (stem).

Marzipan Christmas Leaves

These can be used for all types of Christmas cakes, for the top, base and side decorations. They are good combined with royal icing Christmas roses (see page 152). Also very good to decorate quickly made 'rough'-iced cakes.

1 Holly leaves and berries: colour some marzipan a deep green and roll out on non-stick (waxed) paper. Either use a metal holly leaf cutter; or cut into strips ¼ in (2 cm) wide and 1½ in (4 cm) long. Take a metal nozzle and using the wide round base, cut out 'bites' from the ends and sides to give the leaves. Mark in a vein with a knife. Leave to dry, either flat or over a wooden spoon handle so they become curved. Make berries from red marzipan.

2 Mistletoe and berries: colour some marzipan a paler, more yellow green than for holly and roll out thinly. Using a sharp knife, cut out elongated narrow leaves with a round end and pointed tail. Mark in a vein with a knife. Make berries from natural coloured marzipan, a little larger than holly berries. Leave to dry.

3 Ivy: colour some marzipan a deepish green. Either copy a real ivy leaf or draw your own pattern on card and cut out. Roll out the marzipan and cut out the leaves either freehand or around the patterns. Mark in veins and leave to dry.

These make pretty decorations for large Christmas cakes, used on the top or sides of the cake; they also look good on Christmas biscuits and mini-Christmas cakes.

1 Draw a Christmas tree shape on card or thick paper the size required and cut out. Colour the marzipan a deep green, using a paste colouring for the best deep colours, and roll out to about ¼ in (5mm) thick, on non-stick silicone (waxed) paper. Place the pattern on the marzipan, cut around carefully with a sharp knife and remove. Bend the tips of the branches so they tilt upwards a little.

2 Colour a small amount of marzipan a deep red, using Christmas red paste colouring. Roll out and cut out 'tubs' to complete the trees. Attach by sticking on either with a drop of water or a tiny dab of icing. Leave to dry on non-stick silicone (waxed) paper.

3 Put a little white royal icing into an icing bag fitted with a tiny star nozzle and pipe a small star at the top of the tree and tips of the branches. Add a silver or coloured ball to each star and leave to dry.

Father Christmas

Again, these can be used to decorate the top or sides of a Christmas cake, and will be specially popular with children. Create your own Father Christmas by drawing him as you wish.

1 Draw a simple Father Christmas pattern on card and cut out. Colour some marzipan a bright red and roll out on non-stick silicone (waxed) paper. Position the pattern and cut around the shapes and remove. Cut out a small piece so the tip of the hat stands away from the body.

2 Colour a little marzipan brown, roll out and cut out pieces to fit over Father Christmas's sack. Position. Colour a little marzipan black, roll out and cut out boots. Position over the feet and legs and mark down the centre with a knife to separate the feet.

3 Using white royal icing (page 138) in an icing bag fitted with a small star nozzle, pipe in a band and bobble for his hat, a beard and a trim to the jacket and top of his boots. Add minute dots of black marzipan for his eyes and mark in the arms, etc. with a sharp knife or cocktail stick (toothpick). Leave to dry.

Good decorations for Christmas cakes and biscuits. Use marzipan and paste food colourings.

1 **Robins**: colour some marzipan brown and roll out thinly. Draw a robin on stiff card and cut out. Position on marzipan and cut out. Transfer to non-stick silicone (waxed) paper. Also cut out a wing for each bird.

2 Colour some marzipan red, roll out and cut out a 'red breast' for each robin. Attach to the birds, then put a wing on top and mark in feathers with a knife. Mark in an eye with a cocktail stick (toothpick).

3 **Lanterns**: cut out a lantern pattern on stiff paper. First cut out complete lantern on rolled out yellow marzipan. Then cut out the lantern again on red marzipan with the windows. Press together and leave to dry.

This is the most versatile of icings to add to many types of cake (excluding rich fruit cakes), for complete masking as well as just for the top or sides, and for piping. This basic recipe can be coloured and flavoured limitlessly to complement the cake.

Ingredients

To fill and top a 7 in (18 cm) cake, or coat the top and sides

½ cup (4 oz/100 g) butter or soft tub margarine

1½-2 cups (6-8 oz/175-225 g) icing (confectioner's) sugar, sifted

few drops vanilla essence (extract)

1-2 tablespoons top of the milk or lemon juice

1 Cream the butter or margarine until soft, then beat in the sugar a little at a time, adding a few drops of vanilla and sufficient milk or lemon juice to give a fairly firm but spreading consistency.

2 *To fill a cake:* use just under half the icing and spread evenly over one of the layers. Position the second layer and use the remaining icing to spread over the top.

3 *To cover the top of a cake:* simply spread evenly over the top by putting the icing into the centre of the cake and spreading out from the centre to the edges.

Butter Cream Decorations

he simplest decorations can often produce the most attractive designs. With butter cream the flavour of the icing should either match or contrast with the flavour of the cake, and extra decorations such as toasted nuts, or chocolate matchsticks, give the finishing touch.

1 Spread the butter cream evenly over the top of the cake; with a small palette knife or round-bladed knife work a pattern by running the knife blade from one side to the other of the cake and then back again, slightly overlapping the previous line each time and continuing in the same way all over the top of the cake.

2 A further dimension can be added to this design by turning the cake to right angles of the first lines and then working 4-6 single lines across the first ones at regular intervals of approx. 1 in (2.5 cm). Leave the resulting squares plain or add a decoration to the centres or intersections.

3 To 'swirl' the top of the cake, have the butter cream just a little softer than usual and as soon as it is spread evenly over the top, use the palette knife to swirl the icing with small circular movements, pulling it up into peaks as you complete each swirl. Leave to set. If liked, dust with sifted icing (confectioner's) sugar.

A slightly heavier decoration is more effective on a cake covered with butter cream, and usually the simpler the better. Vary the colour and flavour of the decoration to blend or contrast with the cake and icing. All these decorations can be piped on to a plain un-iced cake.

1 Whirls: put the butter cream into a piping (pastry) bag fitted with a star vegetable nozzle and pipe an even number of whirls round the top of the cake a little in from the edge. Twist each whirl slightly as it is piped and pull off the nozzle quickly to give a neat point. Alternately large and small whirls look good too.

2 Rope Topping: use the same nozzle as above. Stand the cake on some greaseproof (waxed) paper on a turntable or upturned plate and pipe a continuous circle all round the top of the cake about ¾ in (2 cm) in from the edge, piping a twist in the circle at regular intervals. The twists may face inwards or outwards. When set the centre or the whole top of the cake can be lightly dusted with sifted icing (confectioner's) sugar.

3 Scrolls: use a small vegetable nozzle or a large star icing nozzle with a bag filled with butter cream. Mark 6-8 places evenly on top of the cake, each 1-1½ in (2.5-4 cm) in from the edge. Put the nozzle on the point in from the edge and carefully pipe a twisted and curved line out to the edge of the cake, decreasing it in size as you go and finishing off neatly.

Decorating Sides of a Cake

If the sides of a sandwich (layer) or other light cake are to be iced or decorated it is best to do so before touching the top of the cake, so as not to disturb the decoration.

1 Stand the cake on some greaseproof (waxed) paper on a turntable or upturned plate. Brush or spread the sides of the cake (after filling if a layered cake) with jam, jelly, sieved marmalade, lemon or orange curd or butter cream, giving an even but not too thick layer.

2 Put the chosen coating for the sides (toasted coconut, toasted chopped nuts, toasted or plain flaked (ribbed) almonds, chocolate flakes or vermicelli, etc.) on a sheet of greaseproof (waxed) paper. Holding the cake carefully on its side, roll in the coating until well covered. Use a palette knife to cover any gaps. Approx. ¾ cup (3 oz/75 g) chopped nuts or chocolate will coat the sides of a 7-8 in (18-20 cm) cake.

3 For a patterned effect, simply spread a slightly thicker layer of butter cream all round the sides, so there are no thin patches, and then use a serrated icing comb or scraper, fork or palette knife to make a wavy or more definite zigzag design all the way round. It is easier to do this with the cake on a turntable or upturned plate so it can be moved round as you work.

Basket Weave Design

This can be worked in butter cream straight on to a sponge or other light cake; or for fruit cakes in royal icing when it should be piped on to a layer of set marzipan.

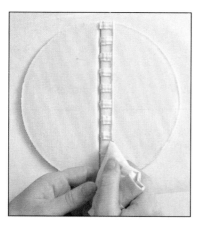

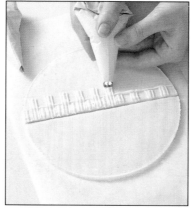

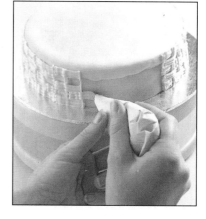

1 You need a basket weave nozzle and a medium to thick writing nozzle (no.3 or 4). Fill the bags, fitted with the nozzles, with butter cream or royal icing. Hold the ribbon nozzle sideways to the cake and at an angle, and pipe three or more short lines the same length as each other, one above the other and with the width of the tip of the nozzle between each one. Pipe a straight vertical line with the writing nozzle along the edge of the three or more ribbon lines.

2 Next, with the ribbon nozzle, pipe three or more straight lines of the same length as the first ones to fill in the gaps, but beginning halfway along the first ones and covering the straight line.

3 Pipe another vertical line at the end of these lines and continue building up first with the ribbon nozzle and then the vertical line until you join up with the start, if you are going round the sides of the cake, or until the top is covered.

Feather Icing

Speed is the essence here for if the top layer begins to set before you complete, the effect will not be so dramatic. Use strongly contrasting colours for the best effect. Glacé icing is used for feathering but melted chocolate can be used for the piped lines.

Glacé Icing

Ingredients

2½ cups (10 oz/300 g) icing (confectioner's) sugar, sifted
2½–4 tablespoons warm water
food colouring and/or flavouring (optional)

1 Put the sugar into a bowl and gradually beat in sufficient water to give a smooth mixture, thick enough to coat the back of a spoon. Extra water or icing (confectioner's) sugar can be added to achieve the correct consistency. Add colourings and/or flavourings. Use at once to cover the top of the cake or stand the covered bowl over a pan of hot water for a short time only.

2 Prepare the sides of the cake first. Remove about one-fifth of the icing and colour strongly to contrast with the base icing; or colour the base icing and leave the rest white. Put the small amount into a greaseproof (waxed) paper icing bag without cutting off the tip or adding a nozzle. Use the base icing to cover the top of the cake. Cut the tip off the icing bag and quickly pipe straight lines across the top of cake at ½–¾ in (1-2 cm) intervals.

3 Quickly take a skewer or point of a knife and draw across the piped lines at right angles about 1 in (2.5 cm) apart. Turn the cake around, then draw the skewer across again between the first lines but in the opposite direction, to complete the feathered effect. Alternatively, pipe a spiral on top of the cake, from the centre to the edge. Draw the skewer from the centre to the edge to divide into quarters, then from the edge to the centre between the first lines.

Royal Icing a Cake

*S*ome people prefer to start with the top and then ice the sides; others start with the sides. The order makes no difference to the finished results. When each layer of icing is dry, any uneven lumps or bumps can be removed by carefully paring away with a very finely serrated long thin knife.

Royal Icing

Ingredients

Sufficient to coat top and sides of a 7 in (18 cm) round cake.
about 4 cups (1 lb/450g) icing (confectioner's) sugar, sifted
2 egg whites (size 2 or 3), beaten until frothy
2 teaspoons lemon juice, strained
1 teaspoon glycerine

1 Beat half the sugar into egg whites. Add lemon juice, glycerine and half remaining sugar, beat until smooth. Beat in enough sugar to stand in soft peaks. Store in airtight container. To ice top of cake: attach cake to cake board with dab of icing. Put some icing in the centre, smooth out with a palette knife. Remove uneven lumps with icing ruler.

2 Stand the cake and board on a turntable. Remove surplus icing from around the sides, rotating the cake and using a palette knife.

3 To *ice square cake sides*: spread some icing on to one side and draw comb towards you. Cut off the icing down the corner in a straight line and also off the top and base of the cake. Repeat with the other two sides when dry. Using an icing ruler, draw it across the cake towards you, evenly, keeping the ruler at an angle of about 30°.

For *round cakes*, apply icing evenly, turning the cake on the turntable. Finish off as for square cakes.

Simple Decorative Edges

Royal icing, which holds its shape so well, is used for these and most other icing decorations. Dots can be worked in a variety of sizes governed by the size of nozzle used. 0 is the very finest, moving up to 4 and larger. A fine vegetable nozzle gives a very big dot.

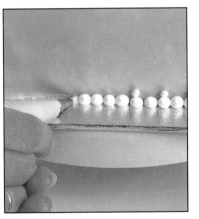

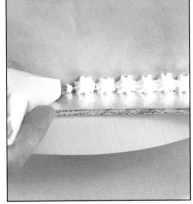

1 Dots: hold the nozzle upright with the tip just touching the surface. Squeeze the bag gently to allow the icing to emerge and at the same time lift the nozzle. Continue squeezing until the size of dot you want is achieved, then remove nozzle with a quick slight down and upward movement. Lift off any 'tail' with a cocktail stick (toothpick).

2 Stars: place a suitable sized star nozzle in the bag and fill with icing. Hold the bag upright and just above the surface. Pipe out the size of star required, then quickly lift off with a down and up movement as for dots. Stars should be kept fairly flat and not pulled up to a point in the centre.

3 Rosettes and whirls: similar to stars but worked in a circular movement. Begin just above the surface, move in a complete circle to enclose the middle. Finish off with a slightly raised point.

Although several types of icing pumps and plastic icing bags complete with connectors are available, it is easiest to use a nozzle with a home-made greaseproof (waxed) paper icing bag, which is inexpensive and easy to make.

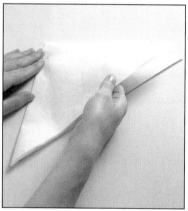

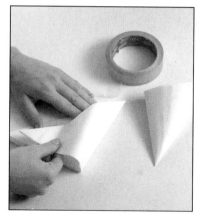

1 Cut a piece of good quality greaseproof (waxed) paper to a 10-12 in (25-30 cm) square then fold in half to form a triangle. Fold the triangle in half to make a smaller triangle and crease the folds firmly.

2 Open out the smaller triangle and fold the bottom half of it up to the folded line, creasing firmly.

3 Continue to fold the bag over once, and then again, still creasing the folds firmly, to give a complete bag. Secure the join with clear sticky tape. When ready to use snip off the tip just sufficiently to hold the nozzle. Many bags can be made at a time and stored until required, tucked into each other.

Decorations of a simple nature can be piped straight on to royal-iced cakes and those covered with rolled out icing.

1 Forget-me-nots: these are made using a fine writing nozzle (no.1 or 2). First stems are piped freehand on to the cake and then leaves; then the flowers are added by making small dots up and down the stems.

2 Lilies of the valley: similar method, the little bells are piped on to the stems. Leaves are also piped. If you feel you can't manage freehand then mark the shapes on the cake using the point of a skewer. Do not draw on with pencil as the lines always show.

3 Daisies: pipe a criss-cross of four short lines for the daisy petals and then pipe a dot or several small dots in the centre. The centre dot can be a different colour to the petals if liked, or the whole flower made in one colour.

Scrolls, Shells and Trellis

These are used for top and base edgings as well as for individual decorations placed on the tops, over the edges and on the sides of cakes. They can be worked to simple and very intricate designs with a little practice.

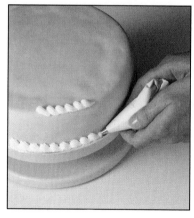

1 Scrolls: use a star or shell nozzle and hold the icing bag filled with royal icing as for a straight line. Keep the nozzle just above the surface. For a question mark shape, begin with a fairly thick head and gradually release the pressure while tailing off to a point. For a twisted scroll, twist the nozzle in a clockwise movement while keeping the shape – the size can be graduated by varying the pressure on the icing bag.

2 Shells: use a star or special shell nozzle. Start in the centre of the shell and first move the nozzle away from you, maintaining an even pressure, then back towards you, exerting a little more pressure for the 'fat' part: allow the icing to tail off and pull off sharply to make a point. Begin the next shell over the point of the previous one to hide it. These can be worked on any edge, or over it, by beginning on top and ending on the side.

3 Trellis: first pipe a series of equidistant parallel straight lines. When dry, pipe another series of parallel lines either at right angles or at a slanting angle to the first lines. To complete a third layer of lines exactly over the first ones. The secret is to have a steady hand and keep the lines absolutely straight and even.

These can be made either using a special leaf piping nozzle or by cutting the tip off a paper icing bag. To do this, fill the bag with royal icing as usual, then press the end flat between the thumb and finger and cut the point off in an inverted letter 'V' like the head of an arrow. For a more intricate leaf, then take out a tiny 'v' from the arrow head itself.

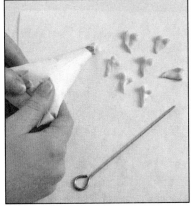

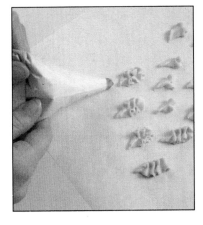

1 Royal icing is generally used, but butter cream leaves can be piped straight on to the cake itself. Begin with the nozzle or paper bag touching the cake (or paper) and the end turning up a fraction. Press gently and as the icing begins to come out of the bag, raise it slightly. Pipe straight on the cake, or onto non-stick silicone (waxed) paper.

2 When the leaf is large enough, break the icing off quickly leaving a point. The bag can be gently twisted or moved up and down to give different shapes and twists to the leaves and the size can be increased by extra pressure. Leave to dry.

3 A variation is to make three overlapping movements for each leaf, pulling the point away sharply after the last one to leave a point. For a leaf edging to a cake, work each leaf separately on the cake, working backwards round the edge so the leaf tips overlap and are left showing. If you have piped leaves onto paper, attach to the cake with a dab of icing when dry.

This is an attractive and fairly simple decoration to add to a cake. It can be worked using a very fine writing nozzle up to a thick one. Lacework is usually piped directly on to a cake, but can also be used to fill in outlines which are then stuck on to the cake with dabs of icing.

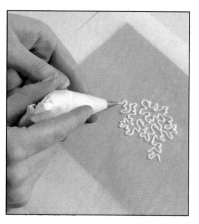

1 Outline or mark the shape to be 'lace-filled' on the top or side of the cake. Fit the icing bag with desired thickness of nozzle and fill the bag with royal icing. Hold the nozzle almost upright and just above the surface so that the icing flows out, and then move the nozzle around backwards and forwards and in all directions, rather like scribbling.

2 Lacework looks good over the edge of a cake too. Mark the shapes by using a cut-out template and outline on the top and side of the cake, then fill in as before. Take care, for as you go over the edge and down the side the icing tends to 'run away' from you if you work too quickly.

3 Lacework shapes: on non-stick silicone (waxed) paper over a drawn pattern, first work an outline with either the same thickness of nozzle or a slightly thicker one, and then fill in with a delicate lacework pattern, keeping the patterns fairly small and close and touching the outline fairly frequently so it can hold together. Leave for at least 12 hours to dry before carefully removing to stick to the cake with a dab of icing.

Piped Fans

hese delicate small shapes are in royal icing piped on non-stick silicone (waxed) paper and when dry, carefully attached to the top or sides of the cake with a tiny dab of icing. Hold the fan with tweezers to make application easier.

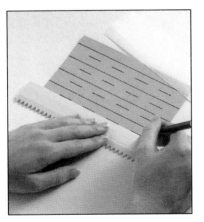

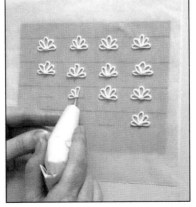

1 On a piece of paper draw a number of lines the length the fan is to be, usually ½-¾ in (1-2 cm), and with enough space and height between each to work the fan. Also draw a line to show the height of the fans. Then place a piece of non-stick silicone (waxed) paper over it and attach. The lines will be your pattern.

2 Fit an icing bag with a fine to medium writing nozzle, and fill the bag with royal icing. Decide on the shape of fan you want and pipe five loops which increase in size to give a fan. Keep the base very straight or it will be difficult to attach to the cake. For a different type of fan, on the first row pipe four shallow loops; on the second row three loops in between the first ones; on the third row pipe two loops, and finish with one loop on top of that. Leave to dry.

3 When the fans are dry, carefully pick up a fan with a pair of tweezers and add a dab of icing to the base of the fan. Attach carefully to the cake, holding it in place if necessary until beginning to dry.

These add interest and extra shapes to cakes. They are usually made from runouts, as in steps 1 and 2, but you can cheat a little and cut them out of fondant or moulding icing (see step 3). Take care, they are very fragile and need gentle handling.

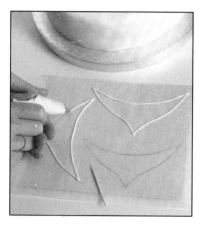

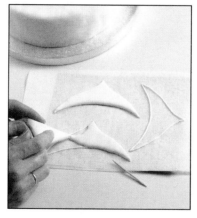

1 On a sheet of paper cut out a corner or curve to fit exactly a square or round cake. Draw a curved shape as in the picture, or any other shape required. Cover this sheet of paper with non-stick silicone (waxed) paper. Using a no.2 writing nozzle and royal icing of your chosen colour, pipe an outline to each of the shapes (always allowing at least two extra), and trim off any joins with a cocktail stick (toothpick), if necessary, so the points are very definite.

2 Thin a little of the icing with lemon juice or egg white and put into a paper icing bag without a nozzle in it and without cutting off the tip. The icing should be thick but just flow enough to settle flat. Cut off the tip of the bag and use to flood the shape, using a cocktail stick (toothpick) to guide the icing into the corners. Leave for 24-48 hours to dry out completely. These collars can be decorated further with piped icing, silver balls, etc.

3 For simple collars, roll out coloured fondant or moulding icing thinly, place a paper pattern on top and cut out. Leave to dry before using.

*B*y this method you can make all sorts of shapes to decorate cakes, and when dry the runouts can themselves be decorated with icing, silver balls, etc. Make sure the runouts are well filled or they will dry out with dips and air bubbles.

1 Draw the shapes you want to fill on a piece of card and cover with a sheet of non-stick silicone (waxed) paper. Using a medium (no. 2) writing nozzle, outline the shape in royal icing and leave to dry partly. Then thin down the icing, using egg white or lemon juice, and put into a paper icing bag without a nozzle. Cut off the tip and use to fill in the shapes, pricking any air bubbles as they appear with a pin.

2 For butterflies, first draw the wings, then, using the writing nozzle, pipe out 'bodies' using an overlapping twisted movement. Leave to dry completely. To assemble: attach a wing to each side of the body with a little icing and then attach a pair of antennae to the head, using cut flower stamen and a dab of icing. Leave to dry and then, if liked, decorate the wings with dots or stars of the same colour or contrasting icing. Leave to dry completely.

3 Other shapes such as hearts, stars, clubs, diamonds, etc. can be made in the same way. When dry, add silver balls and other decorations to small dots or stars piped on to the points of the shapes.

*T*his can be worked in several ways but the idea is to work a series of parallel lines in one direction, then work a second series of parallel lines at right angles to the first ones and when these are dry to pipe a third line exactly over the first ones.

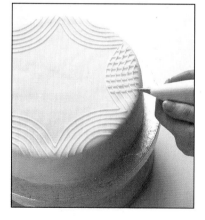

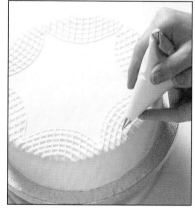

1 On a cake outline the shape to be filled in with trellis using a template and an icing bag fitted with a fine writing nozzle. Remove template and leave to dry.

2 Work a series of lines inside the template line, keeping them equidistant and perfectly straight. Leave to dry completely. Then pipe a series of lines at right angles to the first lines. Carefully lift off any broken or crooked lines, using a fine skewer or cocktail stick (toothpick). Leave to dry completely before proceeding, or if you do make a mistake you will lift off much more then you mean to.

3 Next, pipe another row of lines over the first ones, keeping them exactly straight. Curved and straight lines can be worked with great effect and you can design all sorts of shapes to be filled with trellis.

Curtain Work

This requires a steady hand and a fine writing nozzle but the effect is quite outstanding for a very special cake.

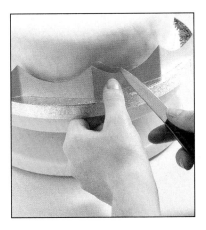

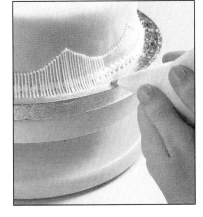

1 First make a template for the curves. Cut a strip of paper about 1 in (2.5 cm) deep which reaches all round the side of the cake. Divide this into equal widths of about 2 in (5 cm) and cut out shallow curves. Open out the strip and place around the sides of the cake so that it touches the board. Make a mark on the cake, using a cocktail stick (toothpick) to show the curves.

2 Using an icing bag fitted with a writing nozzle, pipe a series of dots all round the base of the cake to attach to the board; then using a fine writing nozzle, pipe a series of almost touching tiny dots all round to outline the curves.

3 Using the fine writing nozzle, pipe straight, even lines from the dots on the cake to the board. If it helps, a series of dots can also be worked on the board, to help guide the lines. Keep the curtain work very neat and if even one line is not straight, remove and repeat. Leave to dry completely.

Piped Roses

As with all piped flowers you need a little practice at first, but then they are very simple and can be made very quickly.

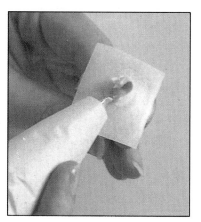 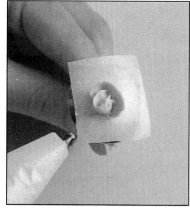 

1 Cut out a quantity of non-stick silicone (waxed) paper squares approx. 1½ in (4 cm). Stick a paper square to an icing nail with a dab of icing for each flower. Fit an icing bag with a petal nozzle and half-fill the bag with a quantity of suitably coloured royal icing. Hold the bag so the thin edge of the nozzle is upwards. Squeezing evenly and twisting the nail at the same time, pipe a tight coil for the centre of the rose.

2 Continue to add petals one at a time but taking each petal only about three-quarters of the way round the flower each time. Begin in a different part of the flower each time to keep the shape even.

3 Work from 3-6 petals for each flower depending on the size you require. They can be worked tightly to form a rosebud or be left more open with loose petals for full-blown flowers. Remove paper square from the icing nail as each rose is made and put on a flat surface to dry for about 24 hours. Once dry, the roses may be stored in an airtight container for several weeks.

Piped Bluebirds

Pretty decorations for christening cakes and other delicate cakes such as wedding and birthday cakes. Make them in any colour you choose.

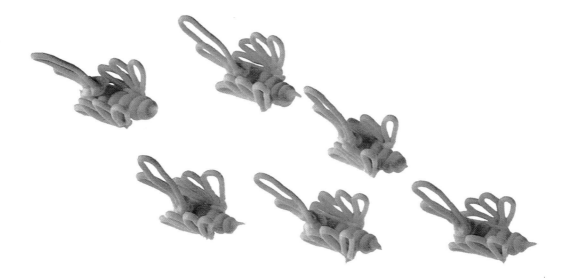

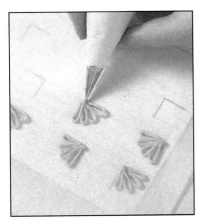

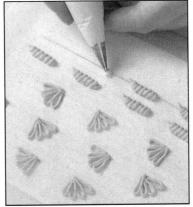

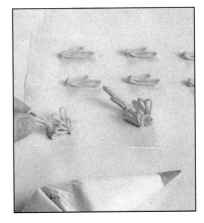

1 On a sheet of paper draw pairs of opposite right angles with lines ½ in (1.5 cm) long. Cover with non-stick silicone (waxed) paper. Using coloured royal icing and a fine writing nozzle (no.1), begin inside one of the angles: pipe up a vertical line and bring back to form the first feather. Fill in the rest of the wing with 3 or 4 more feathers all just touching.

2 For the bodies take a no.2 writing nozzle and pipe out a continuous twisted line for the body a little longer than the wings and finish off with a bulb for the head and a pulled off pointed beak. For tails: pipe first a dot then 2 straight feathers extending outwards from the dot, one slightly shorter than the other. Leave to dry.

3 To assemble: stand the body on non-stick silicone (waxed) paper and attach a wing each side with a dab of icing. Next pipe a dot at the opposite end of the body to the beak and attach a tail with the short feather under the long one. Leave to dry, then attach to the cake with dabs of icing.

These are made using a special petal nozzle. The centres of both flowers are simply finished with a series of dots.

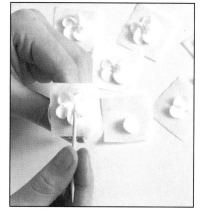

1 Primroses: tint some royal icing pale yellow. Fit an icing bag with a petal nozzle. This is a five-petalled flower with almost heart-shaped petals. Keep the nozzle flat and work each petal separately. Squeezing gently and evenly, take the tip outwards to a point, give a tiny dip towards the centre and then quickly take it out again before bringing it back to the centre and breaking off. Complete the flower and leave to dry.

2 Tint a little royal icing a deep yellow and put into an icing bag fitted with a writing nozzle (no.1 or 2). Use this to pipe a ring of yellow dots in the centre of the primrose, adding one in the centre.

3 Christmas roses: These are worked in white icing and again have a deep yellow centre piped as for primroses. The flower is made in a similar way but the petals are tilted slightly upwards at the edges and rounded to give a 'tea-rose' shape. For lenten lilies the centre of the petals can be tinted mauve, using a fine paint brush and mauve and pink food colourings.

Both these flowers are a little more complicated but the results are very pretty.

1 Violets: the most difficult part is to get a really deep mauve coloured icing for this flower. Work as for a pansy, but make the first four petals much smaller and more pointed. Turn the flower around and pipe a larger elongated petal. Add fine dots of pale green or yellow icing for the stamen.

2 Turn the flower around 180° and work another larger petal to complete it. Leave to dry. Then paint deeper shades of mauve, orange, etc., using liquid food colouring or icing pens. Complete with a few dots of yellow icing for the stamen.

3 Pansies: another five-petalled flower but worked in a different order. Colourings are numerous and usually fairly deep-toned. Fit the icing bag with a petal nozzle and half-fill the bag with coloured royal icing. Pipe two flat, rounded petals, underlapping the second. Then work the next two petals slightly on top of the first two and a little larger, again underlapping the second.

Narcissi and Daisies

Narcissi and daffodils can be worked in a similar way with the petals and centres in shades of yellow, white, cream and orange. Daisies are a simple but effective decoration.

1 Narcissus: this is a flat flower, so begin with the thick edge of the petal nozzle to the centre. Keep the nozzle flat and work each petal separately. Gently squeezing out the appropriately coloured royal icing, take the tip outwards to a point, still keeping it flat, then bring it back towards the centre, twist slightly and break off. This is a six-petalled flower, so work five more petals evenly round to complete it. Leave to dry.

2 For the centre, tint some royal icing yellow or orange and put into an icing bag fitted with a petal nozzle. Pipe a cup right in the centre of the flower by making a complete circle of icing while rotating the nail. Leave to dry. Dots of yellow or orange can be piped into the centre of the cup for the stamen. The top edge of the cup can be carefully painted a deeper orange, using liquid food colouring.

3 Daisies: they can be made in any colour, often with a yellow or deeper shade of the main colour for the centre. Make six or seven petals by holding the petal nozzle upright, with the thick edge at the centre. Simply pipe out petals on the spot, moving round for each one. Using a medium writing nozzle and a contrasting colour, pipe a large dot in the centre. Dry.

These can be made to look absolutely realistic with a little practice. The secret is to press the icing out very thinly, especially at the edges, and to keep the centre narrow, otherwise the flower resembles a cabbage more than a rose!

1 There are two ways of making roses, using moulding or fondant icing. Either roll out thinly on non-stick silicone (waxed) paper and cut out circles of ½-¾ in (1-2 cm), a few at a time and keep them covered with polythene to prevent drying out. Or take tiny pieces of the icing and press each into a circle. The circles get progressively larger for each petal. Press out a tiny one for the centre, so it is very thin, and then roll it up fairly tightly.

2 Press out a second circle of icing thinly and wrap it carefully around, keeping it tight at the base but leaving it looser at the top.

3 Continue to add two, three or four more petals in the same way, each a little larger than the previous one, keeping them thin at the edges and attaching each a little further round than the previous one. If necessary add a dab of water to make them stick. The outer petals can have the tips folded outwards slightly to look more realistic. Trim the base and put to dry on non-stick silicone (waxed) paper for 24-48 hours before attaching to a cake.

A really pretty flower made from fondant or moulding icing, which will grace any cake. It is probably easiest to copy the colours of a real orchid. You need to colour about 3 oz (75 g) fondant or moulding icing a mid-mauve, using mauve and pink colourings; then colour almost half this icing a much deeper mauve. Then colour about 5 oz (150 g) fondant icing deep cream with a touch of egg yellow colouring.

Makes 8-10

1 For each flower take a piece of deep mauve icing and mould it into a narrow tongue shape about 1 in (2.5 cm) long and ⅓ in (1 cm) wide. Using the pale mauve fondant, press out a circle of approx 1¼ in (3 cm) with a wider 'lip' at end. Take several stamens (available from cake decorating shops) and lay on the tongue. Wind the pale mauve piece of icing around it with the 'lip' opposite side to the tongue and bend it back.

2 Use cream fondant to shape five petals each just over 1½ in (4 cm) long and almost ¾ in (2 cm) wide, with the tips being slightly elongated. Put three petals together, bending the tips and sides upwards so they look real, then put the mauve part of the flower on these with the dark mauve tongue touching the cream petals.

3 Take the last two petals and place so they come partly over the top of the flower but they bend off sideways so they don't completely cover the mauve centre. Add a tiny cream tip of icing to each tongue and leave to dry. To complete draw lines and dots on the pale mauve part of the flower.

These look very pretty on any type of celebration cake and can be made in a variety of colours to suit your colour schemes, for these flowers are grown in many different shades.

1 Take 4 pieces of fondant icing about 3 oz (75 g) each and colour the pieces two shades of mauve, one piece cream and the last a deep fuchsia pink. Take 4 or 5 stamens and fold in half to make a bunch. Press out a small circle of mauve fondant and fold round the stamens. Take a second circle a little larger than the first and wrap round it. Leave to dry a little.

2 Roll a contrasting coloured fondant out on non-stick silicone (waxed) paper and cut out elongated petals with a point, as in the picture. Attach one by dampening the end slightly with water, then attach a second petal in the same way.

3 Attach 2 more petals, keeping them equidistant apart. Place each flower carefully in an empty egg box, bending the petals to look realistic, and leave to dry. Repeat, using variations of the coloured fondants.

Teddy Bears

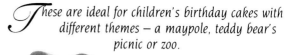

These are ideal for children's birthday cakes with different themes – a maypole, teddy bear's picnic or zoo.

1 Make teddy bears in white, gold or shades of brown fondant or moulding icing and allow from 2 oz (50 g) fondant upwards depending on the size of bear required. Make two rounded legs and put on a piece of non-stick silicone (waxed) paper with the toes just pointing outwards. Make a round body and stand this on top of the feet. Push a cocktail stick (toothpick) through the body so it stands above it by about ¾ in (2 cm).

2 Make a round head with a pointed nose and pinch out two rounded ears with your finger and thumb. Attach to the body standing on the cocktail stick (toothpick). Make two rounded arms from the icing.

3 Attach the arms by dampening with water. Next mark four toes on the feet and hands with a sharp knife. Mark two eyes with a cocktail stick (toothpick) and mark in a smiling mouth. Finish off the head by adding a minute dot of black coloured icing for a nose. Leave to dry.

These two animals can again be added to any child's party cake. The colours can be varied to suit the colour scheme of the cake.

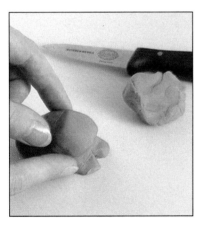

1 Frog: colour the fondant or moulding icing a deep green and reserve about one-third of it. Shape the remainder into a frog's body with one end thicker and bigger than the other. Make a cut into the thicker end of the body and shape the head slightly upwards. Halve the lower piece for two legs and feet. Press the body so it has a large head.

2 Use the remaining fondant to make two back legs and attach. Colour any trimmings a much darker green and cut out tiny dots. Attach these all over the body. Mark toes with a knife and use tiny dots of black or brown coloured fondant for large bulging eyes. Dry.

3 Tortoise: colour about ¾ oz (20 g) fondant icing pale green and about 2 oz (50 g) fondant a greenish-brown colour. Shape the larger piece into a body shell. Make a notch at the front for the head and four small indents for the legs. Shape half the pale green icing into a head and attach. Shape the rest into four feet, then attach. Mark in eyes, nose, mouth and toes with a skewer. With the skewer mark irregular touching circles on the shell with circular shapes in each one.

Useful for children's birthday cakes and all novelty cakes. Colour the rabbits and mice pink, grey or brown.

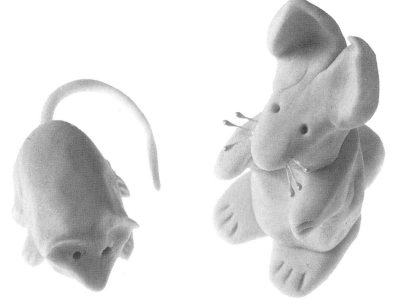

1 *Rabbit:* use about 1½-3 oz (40-75 g) fondant icing and colour all but a tiny piece for his tail, pink, grey or brown. Shape two-thirds into two feet and a body with outstretched paws. Attach the body to the feet.

2 Shape the rest of the icing into a head with two pointed ears and a pointed nose. Attach this to the body using a cocktail stick (toothpick) through the body if necessary to keep it upstanding. Mark two eyes with a cocktail stick and use small pieces of flower stamen for his whiskers. Also mark in toes on his paws. Finally attach a small round white bobtail. Leave to dry.

3 *Mouse:* shape a small piece of coloured fondant into a mouse shape with small feet, a pointed nose and two tiny ears. Mark the eyes with a cocktail stick (toothpick) and the claws on his paws with a knife. Finally add a long thin sausage of the same colour for his tail.

Elephants and Sealions

These look very good on a circus cake with perhaps a clown or some other animals too, or just a selection of elephants and sealions with coloured balls.

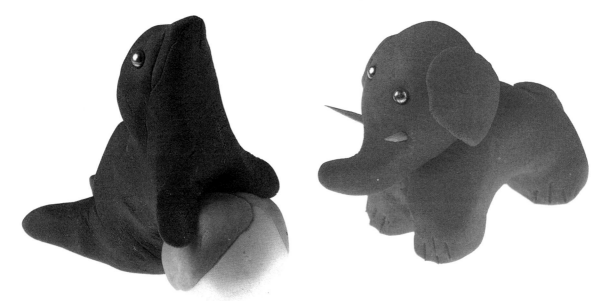

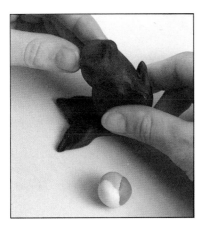

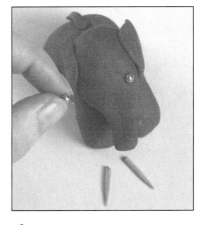

1 Sealions: colour some fondant icing black and a few scraps of icing three colours to make a ball. Mould the black to give a sealion with a pointed head, two flapper front feet, and a tail with a divided tip. Shape him so he stands up and rests on the ball made from the three scraps of fondant. Alternatively let both sealion and ball dry and then balance the ball on his nose, using a piece of cocktail stick (toothpick) and icing to hold it firm.

2 Elephants: these can be any coloured fondant you choose. Shape almost two thirds of the fondant into a body: make a cylinder and bend to form into front and back legs. Split these and form into legs. Take a tiny scrap of fondant for a tail.

3 Shape more icing into a head with a long trunk and attach it to the body using a cocktail stick (toothpick) if necessary to hold it in place. Next shape out two large ears rather like petals when making roses (see page 152) and attach appropriately with a dab of water. Also attach the tail. Add two silver balls for eyes and mark in the toes on all the feet with a knife. Leave to dry.

*C*hildren's cakes can be decorated with dogs and puppies or cats and kittens made to match the shape and colour of your own pets.

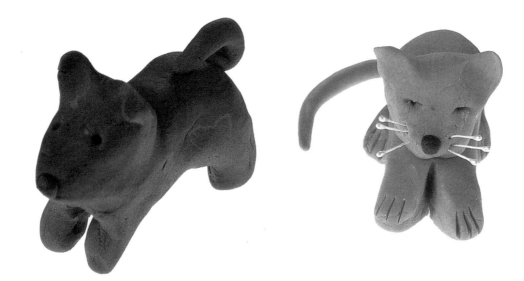

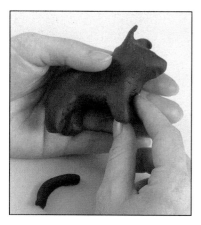

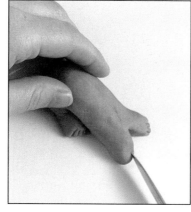

1 Dog: colour about 2-3 oz (50-75 g) fondant icing a suitable 'dog' colour. Remove a tiny piece for his tail and mould the rest into a body with a head with a pointed nose, four legs and two ears. Roll out the reserved piece for a tail and attach. Finally add a tiny dot of black icing or piece of black sweet for a nose and mark in eyes with a cocktail stick (toothpick).

2 Cat: colour the fondant icing any suitable 'cat' colour. Mould two-thirds into a long cylinder and fold under about one-third for the back legs. Split the end so one leg appears each side of the body. Then split the other end in half and shape for the front paws.

3 For the head shape a ball and then press out two pointed ears and a nose. Attach to the body carefully, tipping one of the ears over a little, if liked. Add a tiny dot of black for his nose and small cut pieces of stamen for whiskers. Mark in slit eyes, toes on all four paws, and finally add a thin sausage of fondant for his tail. Dry.

This is a pretty decoration used to add skirts to crinoline lady cakes, twisted frills to petal-shaped cakes and just something a little different to all types of celebration cakes.

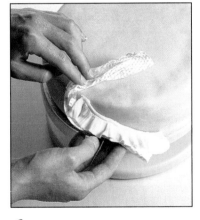

1 Tint a little fondant or moulding icing the desired colour and roll it out thinly on a sheet of non-stick silicone (waxed) paper. Cut into strips about ¾ in (2 cm) wide and then mark a line along the length of each strip about ¼ in (5 mm) from the edge. Do not cut through too deeply.

2 Take a wooden cocktail stick (toothpick) and roll it gently backwards and forwards from side to side below the marked line to thin out the icing. It will make the strip of icing curve around as you go and begin the frilling. Don't make the frills too long or they will break, and work quickly for particularly in hot weather the icing will begin to set and then break before you can get it on to the cake.

3 For a scalloped edge of frilling mark lines on the side of the cake and then pipe a thin line using the same coloured royal icing. Quickly and carefully position the frilling and hold it out from the side of the cake to dry with cotton wool. The joins of frilling are made by moistening the ends of the frills lightly and pressing together and rubbing with the fingertips.

Index